JOKES QUOTES & ANECDOTES

Made Especially
for Citizens with Seniority

To ~~Carol & Jerry~~

PROVERBS 17:22

A. Daniel Goldsmith

Dan Goldsmith

xulon PRESS

Jokes Quotes & Anecdotes
by A. Daniel Goldsmith

Printed in the United States of America

ISBN 9781609577698

Unless otherwise indicated, Bible quotations are taken from the King James Version.

www.xulonpress.com

What they are saying...

"Dan Goldsmith has compiled a volume of pure joy. This book is Novocain! Keep it close when your long hair has given way to a longing for hair. Read it when you can't go out to some new hip joint, because you're getting a new hip joint. I'd take this book over Prozac any day."
Phil Callaway, Speaker and Author of *"Laughing Matters." * Three Hills, AB
(For more humor and laughs visit Phil's website: http://www.laughagain.org)

"Finally, a compendium on humor and life for 'experienced adults!' Dan Goldsmith has done a yeoman's job of gathering far and wide over the years to bring us 'the best of' which I know you'll use in your ministry with older adults when looking for a crowd-breaking, light-hearted or heart-warming moment. And, I think you'll pick it up from time to time just for sheer enjoyment. Feeling low and in need of a good, healthy boost? Read Dan's book! I highly recommend what Dan has compiled and will keep it close to my finger-tips. May you have an ever-laughing life!"
John Coulombe, Pastor, Senior Adults,
First Evangelical Free Church, Fullerton, CA
Leader, Speaker with CASA (Christian Association of Serving Adults)

"Danny Goldsmith and I were young together as boys in Ontario. Now we are older and live far apart, but still friends who love to share memories, and to laugh! We are never too old to laugh. In fact as we get older we should laugh more, having experienced life with its ups and downs, tears and laughter. Someone once asked if Jesus laughed, and an old codger said, 'I think so but He sure fixed me so I could!' Danny's book will help you to say thanks for the gift of laughter... and remember: a merry heart is better than medicine, and many boxes of pills!"
Leighton Ford, President, Leighton Ford Ministries, Charlotte, NC

"Dan Goldsmith is a friend and one of my most respected pastors. Hearty laughter and great humor are some of the refreshment he regularly brings to a conversation or gathering. This book is not just a wonderful resource of quips and funny stories, it is witness to Dan's genuine sense of humor and how skilful he is using fun and light heartedness to bless people. You will thoroughly enjoy this treasure chest of senior's wit and wisdom."
Allen Powles, Pastor to Seniors and Adult Ministries,
Beulah Alliance Church, Edmonton, AB

"*Jokes, Quotes, & Anecdotes* is a helpful book for and about 55+ folks. It is not offensive nor does it downgrade older people. Once you start it, you must turn to the next page for your interest has been caught. This book will give senior leaders and pastors a source book for almost any occasion. You will use it again and again."
Timothy Starr, Pastor to Seniors, The People's Church, Toronto, ON

Dan Goldsmith was born and raised in Chatham, Ontario. He is a graduate of Prairie Bible Institute, Three Hills, AB and Columbia International University, Columbia, SC. He pursued additional studies at Briercrest College & Seminary, Caronport, SK. He began his pastoral ministry in 1958 and has served churches in Alberta and British Columbia until his "first" retirement in 2000. He has served as interim senior pastor in two churches since retiring.

Dan has been commended many times over the years for the humor that he includes in his sermons. He says that he once got so convicted by the amount of humor that he used that he decided to sit down and write out every bit of humorous trivia and all the jokes that he knew. He then threw them into the fire and the fire just roared.

He married his wife, Leona, in 1959 and they have three children and five grandsons. He makes his home in Abbotsford, BC Canada.

Additional copies of this book may be purchased at your local Christian Book Store or from Amazon.com or Barnes & Noble.

DEDICATION

This book is dedicated first and foremost to my wife and companion of 51 years. Leona has heard me tell the same jokes and stories over and over again, but she always smiles or laughs or responds as though she had never heard it before. She also has been most patient with me as I've spent many days, nights and months working on this book. Thanks, sweetheart, for being my great encourager and supporter. I love you! Secondly I want to dedicate this to you, the reader, with the hope and prayer that it will give you a smile or two, lift your spirit and cause you to think.

INTRODUCTION

A few years ago, I was on my way to visit a friend who was hospitalized. I tried to buy a book with some lighter material that would cheer him up. I found a couple of books with humor, but some suggestive and sacrilegious jokes were included. I decided to put together my own collection of humor and anecdotes for seniors. Since then a friend shared with me an article which gave the criteria for good clean humor. I've tried to make this my guide. Here is what it said: "A genuinely good joke is worth a whole lot, but it should be subjected to this test:

- When some woman blushes with embarrassment;
- When some heart carries away an ache;
- When something sacred is made to appear common;
- When a man's weakness provides the cause for laughter;
- When profanity is required to make it funny;
- When a child is brought to tears;
- When not everyone can join in the laughter;
  IT'S A POOR JOKE, DON'T TELL IT!"

This book was put together especially with the *"citizens with seniority"* in mind. If you are in that age bracket, I trust that you are able to laugh at some of the things that happen at the senior stage of life.

A health care publication stated that "humor helps people deal with their disease. When you laugh, your brain releases chemicals that relax your muscles and makes you feel good." [1] It is better to be found guilty of having too much laughter than of having too little. Unfortunately, some people have negative thoughts, critical spirits, and depressed moods. The Bible says that: *"A merry heart doeth good like a medicine: but a broken spirit drieth the bones."* Proverbs 17:22

"When Norman Cousins was given up to die, he determined not to spend his last days in gloom and sadness. He got tapes of all the 'funny people' he could find and watched them for hours. 'Ten minutes of belly-laughing,' said Cousins, 'relieved me of pain for an hour.' He recovered from the illness and went back to work." [2]

In this book you will see that in addition to the humor that I have also included several bits and pieces of information pertinent to seniors and some inspirational thoughts which I trust will remind you that this life is not the only life.

I hope that you will read some things in the following pages that will give you a good "belly laugh." I pray that some of the more serious and inspirational thoughts will make you think about the future and the life that is beyond. Researchers at the University of Michigan have said that: "While the average child laughs 150 times a day, the average adult laughs only 15 times." [3] May the jokes and anecdotes contained in this book help you to be above average.

ACKNOWLEDGMENT

I want to thank my son Dan Jr. Dan has been the one who did the proof reading, correcting and some editing. I want to thank my brother David, who after receiving a copy of this material as a gift on Christmas Day 2009 encouraged me to have it published. Special thanks go to Paul Redekop and to Kay Heppner. Paul has shared stories, bits of humor, etc. with me over the past twenty years. Kay let me read her late husband Herb's journals and files of jokes and anecdotes. And what would I do without my computer mentor? Thanks to Don Dirks for his patience with me re the computer skills, etc. I also want to thank the many relatives and friends, who over the years have shared jokes, stories, and inspirational thoughts with me.

In addition, I have gleaned from books, magazines, speakers, radio, television and the internet. Since most of the material in this book would be followed by the words "anonymous" or "author unknown," I have omitted those words. An author's name is attached only where I had a name. Where I was able to secure permission, credit is given in the endnotes. So to those people who gave permission, and to those whose name appears, but I was unable to secure your permission, and to those whose work is "anonymous" let me say "thank you." I trust that the readers will enjoy your contributions even as I have.

So enjoy the contents.

Dan Goldsmith
August 2010

GETTING SERIOUS ABOUT HUMOR

Laughter is a wonderful coping devise we're given to help us enjoy life's still waters to their fullest and successfully traverse the dangerous currents. Humor is something I can get serious about. It is nothing less than an extravagant gift to be both enjoyed and shared.

I believe it was Billy Graham who said that a keen sense of humor helps us to overlook the unbecoming, understand the unconventional, tolerate the unpleasant, overcome the unexpected, and outlast the unbearable.

The best part of all is that you already received the gift of laughter. Will you use it and share it often today? - Author Unknown

**"You don't stop laughing because you grow old.
You grow old because you stop laughing."**

MY AFFLICTION IS OLD AGE

Thought I'd let my doctor check me
Cause I didn't feel quite right
All those aches and pains annoyed me,
And I couldn't sleep at night.

He could find no real disorder,
But he wouldn't let it rest
What with Medicare and Blue Cross,
It wouldn't hurt to do some tests.

To the hospital he did send me,
Though I didn't feel that bad
He arranged for them to give me
Every test that could be had.

I was fluoroscoped and cystoscoped,
My aging frame displayed,
Stripped upon an ice-cold table
While my gizzards were x-rayed.

I was checked for worms and parasites,
For fungus and the crud,
While they pierced me with long needles
Taking samples of my blood.

Doctors came to check me over,
Probed and pushed and poked around
And to make sure I was living,
They wired me for sound.

They have finally concluded
Their results have filled a page
What I have will someday kill me
My affliction is OLD AGE!

**"At age twenty, we worry about what others think of us. At forty, we
don't care what they think of us. At sixty, we discover that they
haven't been thinking about us at all."** - Jack Falson

"You know that you are getting older when the candles cost more than the cake." - Bob Hope

HOW OLD ARE YOU?

When my grandson asked me how old I was, I teasingly replied, "I'm not sure."

"Look in your underwear, Grandma," he advised. "Mine says I'm four."

STOP – ACTS 2:38

Having just returned home from an evening church service, the elderly woman was startled by an intruder in the act of robbing her home. "STOP Acts 2:38," she yelled. *(Repent and be baptized, every one of you in the name of Jesus Christ...)*

The burglar stopped in his tracks. The woman calmly called the police and explained what she had done. As the officer cuffed the man to take him in, he asked the burglar, "Why did you just stand there? All the old lady did was yell a scripture at you."

"Scripture?" replied the burglar, "she said she had an axe and two 38's!"

"Families are like fudge, mostly sweet with a few nuts."

AGING IS A MATTER OF PERSPECTIVE

While waiting for my first appointment in the reception room of a new dentist, I noticed his certificate, which bore his full name. Suddenly, I remembered that a tall boy with the same name had been a class mate in my high school class some 40 years ago.

Upon seeing him, however, I quickly discarded any such thought. This balding, grey-haired man with the deeply lined face was too old to have been my classmate.

After he had examined my teeth, I asked him if he had attended the local high school.

"Yes," he replied.

"When did you graduate?" I asked.

He answered, "In 1970."

"Why, you were in my class!" I exclaimed.

He looked at me closely and then asked, "What did you teach?"

"Age is a matter of mind. If you don't mind, it doesn't matter."

I'M AWFULLY WELL FOR THE SHAPE I'M IN

There's nothing whatever the matter with me;
I'm just as healthy as I can be.
I have arthritis in both of my knees;
And when I talk, I talk with a wheeze.

My pulse is weak, and my blood is thin,
But I'm awfully well for the shape I'm in.
Arch supports I have for my feet,
Or I wouldn't be able to walk on the street.

Sleep is denied me night after night,
And every morning I look a sight.
My memory is failing; my head's in a spin
But I'm awfully well for the shape I'm in.

The moral is, as this tale we unfold,
That for you and me who are growing old,
It is better to say, "I'm fine," with a grin,
Than to let them know the shape we're in.

**"Old age is having too much room in the house
and not enough in the medicine cabinet."**

IF THEY HAD A SECOND CHANCE

Several people in their 90's were once interviewed and asked what they would do differently if they had the opportunity to live their lives again. The top three responses were:
  (1) I would take more risks.
  (2) I would do more reflecting.
  (3) I would do more things that would continue after I am gone.

A YOUNG UPSTART SPEAKS

A ninety-eight year old gent lived up on the side of the mountain. His seventy-eight year old son wanted him to move down from the mountain. The ninety-eight year old said to his fifty-seven year old grandson, "It's not that I mind movin', it's jest that I hate to have a young upstart tellin' me what to do."

"I like the dreams of the future better than the history of the past."
- Thomas Jefferson

"The trick is growing up without growing old." - Casey Stengel

JOKES ABOUT OLD FOLKS

To tell a joke about old folks is really not a sin,
So long as it would maybe fit yourself or one of kin.

The best of fun may be a pun, a story bout yourself
To laugh at ills and taking pills, we could be on the shelf.

So it's o.k. to have your say and laugh at this thing age,
It helps us deal with what is real, and loving this life stage.
- A. Daniel Goldsmith

SHE WAS A SMART WOMAN

A lawyer started to get real pushy while cross-examining a little old lady. The elderly lady remained quite calm. Finally the lawyer said, "You say you had no education. You answered my questions smartly enough."

The little old lady said, "You don't have to be a scholar to answer silly questions."

THE DOCTOR'S COMMENTS

Morris, an 82 year old man went to the Doctor to get a physical. A few days later the doctor saw Morris walking down the street with a gorgeous young lady on his arm. A couple of days later the doctor spoke to the man and said, "You're really doing great aren't you?"

Morris replied, "Just doing what you said, Doctor: 'Get a hot mamma and be cheerful'."

The Doctor said, "I didn't say that. I said you got a heart murmur. Be careful."

SING HYMNS WHEN YOU'RE 65

A woman who was past the age of 65 spoke to her pastor and said: "I'll be so happy when all of these younger ones are 65 and then they will enjoy singing the hymns."

"Lady," said the pastor, "if they sing choruses now, they will be singing choruses after they are 65. You sing hymns because that is what you sang when you were young."

"There are three stages to life: youth, middle age, and 'My you're looking good'!"

HEARING PROBLEM

A concerned husband, who worried that his wife's hearing was failing, called her doctor to make an appointment to have her ears checked. The doctor said that the earliest he could see her would be two weeks later. However, there's a simple test the husband could do to get some idea of the dimensions of the problem.

"Here's what you do," said the doctor. "Start about 40 feet away from her, and speak in a normal conversational tone and see if she hears you. If not, go to 30 feet, 20 feet, and so on until you get a response."

So that evening she's in the kitchen cooking dinner, and he's in the living room thinking "I'm about 40 feet away... let's see what happens."

"Honey, what's for supper?"

No response. So he moves to about 30 feet away.

"Honey, what's for supper?"

No response. He then moves into the dining room, about 20 feet away.

"Honey, what's for supper?"

No response. At the kitchen door, ten feet away.

"Honey, what's for supper?"

Still no response. Finally, he walks right up behind her and says

"Honey, what's for supper?"

She finally screams, "For the fifth time, WE'RE HAVING FRIED CHICKEN!"

SWEETHEART, HONEY, PUMPKIN

An elderly gent was invited to his old friends' home for dinner one evening. His friend had been married 70 years and he was impressed by the way that his buddy preceded every request to his wife with endearing terms – Honey, My Love, Darling, Sweetheart, Pumpkin, etc. While the wife was in the kitchen, the man leaned over and said to his host, "I think its' wonderful that, after all these years, you still call your wife those loving pet names."

The old man hung his head. "I have to tell you the truth," he said, "I forgot her name about 10 years ago."

"The first sign of old age is when you hear snap, crackle, and pop and it isn't your cereal."

THANKFUL SENIORS

At a nursing home in Florida, a group of senior citizens were sitting around talking about their aches and pains. "My arms are so weak I can hardly lift this cup of coffee," said one.

"I know what you mean. My cataracts are so bad I can't even see my coffee," replied another.

"I can't turn my head because of the arthritis in my neck," said a third, to which several nodded weakly in agreement.

"My blood pressure pills make me dizzy," another contributed.

"I guess that's the price we pay for getting old," winced an old man as he slowly shook his head. Then there was a short moment of silence.

"Well it's not that bad," one woman cheerfully said, "thank God we can still drive."

"God promises a safe landing, not a calm passage."

WHAT A DIFFERENCE ONE CENTURY MAKES

1. The average life expectancy in the US was 47 years.

2. Only 14% of the homes in the US had a bath tub.

3. Only 8% of the homes had a telephone. A three minute call from Denver to New York City cost $11.00.

4. There were only 8,000 cars in the US and only 144 miles of paved roads.

5. The maximum speed limit in most cities was 10 mph.

6. Alabama, Mississippi, Iowa and Tennessee were each more heavily populated than California. With a mere 1.4 million residents, California was only the 21st most populous state in the Union.

7. The tallest structure in the world was the Eiffel Tower in France.

8. The average wage in the US was 22 cents an hour.

9. The average US worker made between $200 and $400 per year.

10. A competent accountant could expect to earn $2,000 per year, a dentist $2,500 per year, a veterinarian between $1,500 and $4,000 per year, and a mechanical engineer about $5,000 per year.

11. More than 95% of all births in the US took place at home.

12. Ninety percent of all US physicians had no college education. Instead, they attended medical schools, many of which were condemned in the press and by the government as "substandard."

13. Sugar cost 4 cents a pound. Eggs were 14 cents a dozen.

14. Coffee cost 15 cents a pound.

15. Most women only washed their hair once a month and used Borax or egg yolks for shampoo.

16. The five leading causes of death in the US were (in order of frequency):
    a. Pneumonia and Influenza
    b. Tuberculosis
    c. Diarrhea
    d. Heart disease
    e. Stroke

17. The American flag had 46 stars, New Mexico, Arizona, Alaska and Hawaii hadn't been admitted to the Union yet.

18. The population of Las Vegas, Nevada was 30.

19. Crossword puzzles, canned beer, and iced tea hadn't been invented yet.

20. There was no Mother's Day or Father's Day.

21. One in ten US adults could not read or write.

22. Only 6% of all Americans had graduated from high school.

23. Marijuana, heroin and morphine were all available over the counter at corner drug stores. According to one pharmacist, "heroin clears the complexion, gives buoyancy to the mind, regulates the stomach, and the bowels, and is in fact a perfect guardian of health."

24. Eighteen percent of all households in the US had at least one full-time servant or domestic.

25. There were about 230 reported murders in the entire US.

"For the ignorant, old age is as winter, for the learned, it is a harvest." - Jewish Proverb

A FEW OF MY FAVORITE THINGS
(To the tune of "My Favorite Things")

Maalox and nose drops and needles for knitting
Walkers and handrails and new dental fittings,
Bundles of magazines tied up with string,
These are a few of my favorite things.

Cadillacs, cataracts, hearing aids, glasses
Polident, Fixodent, false teeth in glasses,
Pacemakers, golf carts and porches with swings,
These are a few of my favorite things.

When the pipes leak, when the bones creak
When the knees go bad,
Then I remember my favorite things,
And then I don't feel so bad.

Hot tea and crumpets, and corn pads for bunions,
No spicy hot food no food cooked with onions
Bathrobes and heat pads and hot meals they bring,
These are a few of my favorite things.

Back Pains, confused brains, and no fear of sinning,
Thin bones and fractures and hair that is thinning,
And we won't mention our short shrunken frames
When we remember our favorite things.

When the joints ache, when the hips break,
When the eyes grow dim,
Then I remember the great life I've had,
And then I don't feel so bad.

TIMES HAVE CHANGED

Nancy Reagan tells the story of how President Ronald Reagan was once challenged by a college student who said it was impossible for Reagan's generation to understand his. "You grew up in a different world," the student said. "Today we have television, jet planes, space travel, nuclear energy, computers...."

Taking advantage of a pause in the student's litany, President Reagan said, "You're right. We didn't have those things when we were young. We invented them."

"Don't wait for the hearse to take you to church."

**"You need to forget all the health foods.
You need all the preservatives you can get."**

CHILD'S VIEW OF RETIREMENT

After the Christmas break, the teacher asked her young pupils how they spent their holidays. One little boy's reply went like this:

"We went to Arizona to visit my grandparents. We always used to spend Sundays with Grandma and Grandpa. They used to live close to us in a big brick house, but Grandpa got retarded and they moved to Arizona. They live in a park with a lot of other retarded people. They all live in tin huts. They ride tricycles that are too big for me. They all go to a building they call the wrecked hall, but it is fixed now. They do exercises but not very well. There is a swimming pool, but I guess nobody teaches them how to swim. They just stand there in the water with their hats on.

My Grandma used to bake cookies for me, but nobody cooks there. They all go to restaurants that are fast and have discounts. When you come into the park there is a doll house with a man sitting in it. He watches all day so they can't get out without him seeing them. I guess everybody forgets who they are because they all wear badges with their names on them. Grandma says that Grandpa worked hard all his life to earn his retardment. I wish they would move back home, but I guess the man in the doll house won't let them out."

RECENTLY RETIRED

A fairly recent retiree confessed that he was tired of his retirement. He said: "I wake up in the morning with nothing to do, and by bedtime I have it only half done."

WINTER IN WINNIPEG

It's winter here in Winnipeg
And the gentle breezes blow
At ninety-seven kilometers
And thirty-five below.

Oh, how I love my Winnipeg
When the snow's up to your butt
You take a breath of winter
And your nose gets frozen shut.

Yes, the weather here is wonderful
Seventy years, I've been around
I could never leave my Winnipeg
Cause I'm frozen to the ground

11

"An old-timer is one who remembers when we could buy a pound of steak for forty-nine cents, but forgets that we had to work an hour to earn the forty-nine cents."

THE END IS NEAR

A retired Baptist pastor and a retired Methodist pastor, both residents of a Baptist nursing home, were sitting out in front of their home holding up a sign that said, "The End is Near! Turn yourself around now before it's too late!" They planned to hold up the sign to each passing car.

"Leave us alone, you religious nuts!" yelled the first driver as he sped by.

From around the curve they heard a big splash. "Do you think," said one of the pastors to the other, "that maybe we should put up a sign that simply says 'bridge out'?"

SURPRISES

While she was enjoying a transatlantic ocean trip, Billie Burke, the famous actress, noticed that a gentleman at the next table was suffering from a bad cold.

"Are you uncomfortable?" she asked sympathetically. The man nodded. "I'll tell you what to do for it," she offered. "Go back to your stateroom and drink lots of orange juice. Take two aspirins. Cover yourself with all the blankets you can find. Sweat the cold out. I know just what I'm talking about. I'm Billie Burke from Hollywood."

The man smile warmly and introduced himself in return. "Thanks," he said, "I'm Dr. Mayo of the Mayo Clinic."

"The trouble with retirement, I'll tell you in a rhyme, is when you take your coffee break you're wasting your own time."

COULDN'T TELL THE DIFFERENCE

To help Grandpa lose weight, I told Grandma that she should switch to lower-fat foods, including skim milk. When she said that Grandpa would drink only whole milk, I suggested that she keep a milk container that says whole milk and keep filling it with skim milk. This worked for quite some time, until Grandpa asked one morning whether the milk was okay.

"Sure, it's fine," said Grandma. "Why do you ask?"

"Well," said Grandpa, "according to the expiration date, this milk expired nine months ago!"

"Old age is when your former classmates are so grey, wrinkled and bald that they don't recognize you." - Bennett Cerf

WHEN I'M AN OLD LADY

When I'm an old lady, I'll live with my kids,
And make them so happy, just as they did.
I want to pay back all the joy they've provided,
Returning each deed, oh they'll be so excited.

I'll write on the wall with reds, whites and blues,
And bounce on the furniture wearing my shoes.
I'll drink from the carton and then leave it out,
I'll stuff all the toilets and oh, how they'll shout.

When they're on the phone and just out of reach,
I'll get into things like sugar and bleach.
Oh, they'll snap their fingers and then shake their head,
And when that is done I'll hide under the bed.

When they cook dinner and call me to meals,
I'll not eat my green beans or salads congealed.
I'll gag on my okra, spill milk on the table,
And when they get angry, run fast as I'm able.

I'll sit close to the TV, through the channels I'll click,
I'll cross both my eyes to see if they stick.
I'll take off my socks and throw one away,
And play in the mud til the end of the day.

And later in bed, I'll lay back and sigh,
And thank God in prayer and then close my eyes,
And my kids will look down with a smile slowly creeping,
And say with a groan, "She's so sweet when she's sleeping!"

"Don't let aging get you down. It's too hard to get back up."

AN ANCIENT TIME PIECE

My grandpa was a farmer and did not own a watch. When he went out into the field to work, he did what Alexander the Great used to do. To tell the time, Alexander wrapped cloths around his wrist and then soaked them in water. During the day, he would touch the cloths and determine the hour by the relative dryness of the material. That's how we got "Alexander's Rag Time Band."

**"Time is a great healer.
That's why they make you wait so long in a doctor's office."**

FIFTY YEARS OF MARRIAGE

Fifty years of wedded bliss
Did it start with that first kiss,
Or did it start when both of you
Said "I will" or yes "I do?"

I think it started long before
With One above that we adore,
For from the heart of God above
He placed that little spark of love.

He had His plan made long ago
Before each other you did know,
That you would be a man and wife
Enjoying fifty years of life.
- A. Daniel Goldsmith

**"The worth of a man's life cannot be measured in years,
achievements, or in acquiring fame, but only in how
he has invested it in eternity."** - Dick Innes

A HEART ATTACK

A married couple spent many enjoyable days together in their luxurious boat. The husband was the one that was always behind the wheel operating the boat. He got to thinking one day and became concerned as to what might happen if he should have a heart attack. So he said to his wife, "Please take the wheel, dear. Pretend that I am having a heart attack. You must get the boat safely to shore." She navigated well and drove the boat to shore, and docked the same.

Later that afternoon, the wife walked into the living room where her husband was watching the sports channel. She sat down beside him, switched the TV off, and said to him, "Please go into the kitchen, dear. Pretend that I'm having a heart attack. You must set the table, cook the dinner, and wash the dishes."

**"Old age is that time of life when you know all the answers
and nobody asks you the questions."**

"When your memory goes, forget it."

ONE EXCEPTION

My false teeth fit me dandy,
My hearing aid's just fine,
My glasses come in handy,
But I sure do miss my mind.

"Look at the bright side: No matter how old you are, you're younger than you'll ever be again." - Bob Orben

TO BE SIX AGAIN

A man asked his wife what she'd like for her birthday. "I'd love to be six again," she replied. On the morning of her 65th birthday, he got her up bright and early and off they went to a local theme park. What a day! He put her on every ride in the park: the Death Slide, the Screaming Loop, and the Wall of Fear – everything there was! Wow!

Five hours later she staggered out of the theme park, her head reeling and her stomach upside down. They went to McDonald's where her husband ordered her a Big Mac along with extra fries and a refreshing chocolate shake. Then it was off to a movie, and hot dogs, popcorn, Pepsi Cola and M&M's. What a fabulous adventure!

Finally she wobbled home with her husband and collapsed into bed. He leaned over and lovingly asked, "Well, dear, what was it like being six again?"

One eye slowly opened, and the wife said, "You idiot, I meant my dress size."

The moral of this story, even when the man is listening, he's still going to get it wrong.

THINGS YOU SHOULD HAVE LEARNED BY MIDDLE AGE

1. If you're too open-minded, your brains will fall out.
2. Age is a very high price to pay for maturity.
3. Opportunities always look bigger going than coming.
4. Artificial intelligence is no match for natural stupidity.
5. It is easier to get forgiveness than permission.
6. For every action, there is an equal and opposite government program.
7. Bills travel through the mail at twice the speed of checks.
8. Laughter is a tranquilizer with no side effects.
9. A balanced diet is a cookie in each hand.
10. Never before has the future so rapidly become the past.

"Aging seems to be the only way to live a long time."

**"Middle age is when broadness of the mind
and narrowness of the waist change places."**

WILL YOU MARRY ME?

Two elderly people were living in a Florida mobile home park. He was a widower and she a widow. They had known one another for a couple of years.

One evening there was a community supper in the activity center. These two were at the same table, across from one another. As the meal went on, he made a few admiring glances at her and finally gathered up his courage to ask her, "Will you marry me?"

After about six seconds of 'careful consideration,' she answered, "Yes! Yes, I will!"

The meal ended and with a few more pleasant exchanges. They went to their respective places. The next morning, he was troubled. Did she say "Yes" or did she say "No?" He could not remember. Try as he would, he just could not remember her answer.

With trepidation, he went to the telephone and called her. First, he explained to her that he didn't remember as well as he used to. Then he reviewed the lovely evening they had the night before. As he gained a little more courage, he inquired of her, "When I asked if you would marry me, did you say 'Yes' or did you say 'No'?"

He was delighted to hear her say, "Why I said 'Yes, Yes I will' and I meant it with all my heart." Then she continued, "I am so glad that you called, because I couldn't remember who had asked me."

**"The advantage that age has over youth is that
youth knows nothing about being old, whereas
the old know all about being young."**

HOW Y'ALL FEELING?

The doctor in a small North Carolina clinic asked the weather-beaten mountaineer how he was feeling.

"Well… it's like this," drawled the man. "I'm still a-kickin, but I ain't raisin no dust."

**"Some of those old codgers who keep complaining that things are not
what they used to be always forget to include themselves."**

"The milk of human kindness should never be allowed to curdle."

SENIORS ARE NOT RESPONSIBLE

Senior citizens are sometimes criticized for every conceivable deficiency of the modern world, real or imaginary. We take responsibility for all we have done and do not blame others.

But, upon reflection, we would like to point out that it was NOT the senior citizens who took

> The melody out of music
> The pride out of appearance
> The romance out of love
> The commitment out of marriage
> The responsibility out of parenthood
> The togetherness out of the family
> The learning out of education
> The service out of patriotism
> The religion out of school
> The golden rule from rulers
> The nativity scene out of cities
> The civility out of behavior
> The refinement out of language
> The dedication out of employment
> The prudence out of spending, or
> The ambition out of achievement.

And we certainly are NOT the ones who eliminated patience and tolerance from personal relationships and interactions with others!

"If you look like your passport photo, you probably need the trip."

TOP TEN SIGNS THAT YOU ARE GETTING OLDER

- Your arms are almost too short to read the newspaper.
- You no longer think of the speed limits as a challenge.
- You buy a compass for the dash of your car or truck.
- Your back goes out more than you do.
- You can't remember the last time you lay on the floor to watch TV.
- People call at 9:00pm and ask, "Did I wake you?"
- You quit trying to hold your stomach in, no matter who walks into the room.
- You have a party and the neighbors don't even realize it.
- Your ears are hairier than your head.
- You've heard all this before.

"Many seniors are kind, polite, and sweet-spirited until you try to sit in their pew."

COLD FEET

Did you ever go to bed at night and crawl beneath the sheet
    To have your slumber ruined by a pair of icy feet?
There's many a poor husband who groans in deep despair
    When he finds beneath the covers lies a two-foot Frigidaire.

The land of nod is sabotaged, gone are the dreams he'd cherish,
    For how can man get forty winks when he's about to perish?
What is the use of counting sheep, it's just a waste of breath,
    Those poor defenseless animals would simply freeze to death.

It's bad enough to try to rest where heated comfort lacks,
    But oh, the shivering torture of a chilled foot in one's back.
No male on earth can rise at morn with spirits gay and bright,
    When he's been thus imprisoned in cold storage all the night.

The little wife who shares his bed may have a heart of gold,
    But why did nature spoil the job with feet so bitter cold?
There's far more frigid temperature in a woman's single toe
    Than there is in Arctic circles where it's forty-five below.

Why don't some brilliant scientists invent an anti-freeze
    To bring the circulation back below my lady's knees?
Still there's one consolation if you'd check upon it, men,
    Be glad your spouse has but two feet, instead of nine or ten.

"Nothing is more responsible for the good old days than a poor memory."

SIGNING WILLS

An attorney prepared wills for an elderly couple who had been somewhat apprehensive about discussing death. When they arrived to sign the documents, the attorney ushered the couple into his office and with the wills there on the table waiting to be signed, he said to them, "Which one of you wants to go first?"

TAXI METER

Question: How is life like a taxi-cab?
Answer: The meter keeps going whether you're going somewhere or just standing still.

"When you're through changing, you're through." - Bruce Barton

THE SNORING HUSBAND

The day he came a-wooing, before I was his wife,
I used to think it would easy be with him to spend my life.

His speech was oh so gentle, so tall and straight was he,
I never dreamed how terrible he'd prove some day to be.

I never dreamed I'd wake at night to give his ribs a whack,
With "Darling, please turn over, you're sleeping on your back".

When life was all before us, and our single path uphill,
I never dreamed the time would come I'd wish his voice was still.

And when "for better or for worse" to cling to him I vowed,
I never dreamed so nice a man could make a noise so loud.

All night long I elbow him, until he's blue and black,
And say, "Turn over darling please, you're sleeping on your back."

At times it's like a whistle's shriek, at times a grunt and groan,
Or like a buzz-saw at a knot, until a fuse is blown.

Then comes a second's silence when I think he must be dead,
To find he's merely paused to start full steam ahead.

And this must last my life-time through, for how can I forsake,
This ghastly creature fast asleep, who is so nice awake.

SHOPPING ONLINE

I was visiting my grandmother who was attempting to make an online purchase with her computer. I could not believe my eyes when I saw her putting her credit card into her floppy drive and pulling it out very quickly. I inquired as to what she was doing. She said she was shopping on the Internet. They had asked for a credit card number, so she was doing the ATM "thingy."

WANTS TO PLAY A MUSICAL INSTRUMENT

Papa had always wanted to learn to play a musical instrument. After looking at flutes, dulcimers and recorders, he spotted a shiny, one-stringed instrument in another aisle. He thought it was a mouth harp. He put it to his lips, and much to the amusement of other shoppers, twanged a few notes on it. His grandson, who was watching from a distance came up and whispered in his ear, "Papa, I hate to tell you this, but you're trying to play a cheese slicer."

"Traveling isn't as much fun when all of the historical sites are younger than you are."

HORSEBACK RIDING

"My grandfather is 95 years old and every day he goes horseback riding, except during the month of July."

"Why not during July?" I asked.

"Because that is when the man who puts him on the horse goes on his vacation."

"I'm suffering from Mallzheimer's disease. I go to the mall and forget where I parked my car."

OLD AGE IS GOLDEN

"Old age is golden," I've heard it said,
But sometimes I wonder when I go to bed;
I put my ears in a drawer, my teeth in a cup,
My eyes on a table, until I wake up.
Ere sleep dims my eyes, I say to myself
Is there anything else I should lay on the shelf?
- Charles Lane

"An old-timer is one who will tell you that Cod Liver Oil and Castor Oil were the 'cure-all' drugs of the day." - A. Daniel Goldsmith

GETTING FORGETFUL

Three sisters ages 92, 94 and 96 live in a house together. One night the 96 year old fills the bathtub with water. She puts her foot in, pauses, and yells down the stairs, "Was I getting in or out of the bath?"

The 94 year old yells back, "I don't know, I'll come up and see." She starts up the steps and pauses, "Was I going up the stairs or down?"

The 92 year old is sitting at the kitchen table having tea listening to her sisters. Shaking her head she says, "I sure hope I never get that forgetful," and knocks on wood for good measure. She then yells, "I'll come up and help both of you as soon as I see who's at the door."

"You are young at any age if you are planning for tomorrow."

THE OLD DAYS

"I can't figure it out," said the small boy, trying to get his father to help him with his arithmetic lesson. "If a carpenter was paid three dollars a day, how much did he earn in four days?"

"No wonder you can't figure it out!" exclaimed the father. "That's not arithmetic – that's ancient history!"

"You enter a new phase of life at 65, but with it come fallen arches, arthritis, cataracts, and the tendency to repeat yourself."

THANK GOD THAT I'M ME

When my luck seems all gone, and I'm down in the mouth,
When I'm stuck in the north and I want to go south;
When the world seems a blank and there's no one to love,
And it seems even God's not in Heaven above.
I've a cure for my grouch and it works like a shot,
I just think of the things I am glad that I am not:
> A bird in a cage, a fish in a bowl
> A pig in a pen, a fox in a hole
> A bear in a pit, a wolf in a trap
> A fowl on a spit, a rug on a lap
> A horse in a stable, a cow in a shed
> A plate on a table, a sheet on a bed
> A case on a pillow, a bell on a door
> A branch on a willow, a mat on the floor.
Then my blues disappear when I think what I've got,
And quite soon I've forgotten the things I have not,
When I think of the hundreds of things I might be,
I get down on my knees and thank God that I'm me.
- Elsie Janis

THREE AGES OF LIFE ALL AT ONCE

A person is really in three different ages all at once:

- THE CHRONOLOGICAL AGE – determined by the number of years.
- THE BIOLOGICAL AGE – determined by the condition and state of the body.
- THE PSYCHOLOGICAL AGE – determined by how old a person feels and acts.

"As God adds years to your life, let Him add life to your years."

21

"Though our outward man perish, yet the inward man is renewed day by day." II Corinthians 4:16

HOW OLD IS OLD?

"How old is old?" Sherwood Wirt answered his question, "Old is older than me."

SIR WINSTON CHURCHILL INTERVIEWED

Sir Winston Churchill was interviewed and asked, "If you could live your life again, what would you want to be?"

With a twinkle in his eye, Churchill replied: "Mrs. Churchill's next husband."

THE CLOTHESLINE SAID SO MUCH

A clothesline was a news forecast to the neighbors passing by,
There were no secrets you could keep, when clothes were hung to dry.
It also was a friendly link for neighbors always knew,
If company had stopped on by to spend a night or two.

For then you'd see the fancy sheets and towels out on the line,
You'd see the company tablecloths with intricate design.
The line announced a baby's birth to folks who lived inside,
As brand new infant clothes were hung so carefully with pride.

The ages of the children could so readily be known,
By watching how the sizes changed, you'd know how much they'd grown.
It also told when illness struck, as extra sheets were hung,
Then nightclothes, and a bathrobe, too, haphazardly were strung.

It said, "Gone on vacation now" when lines hung limp and bare,
It told "We're back!" when full lines sagged with not an inch to spare.
New folks in town were scorned upon if wash was dingy gray,
As neighbors raised their brows, and looked disgustedly away.

But clotheslines now are of the past for dryers make work less,
Now what goes on inside a home is anybody's guess.
I really miss that way of life, it was a friendly sign
When neighbors knew each other best by what hung on the line"

"Wholesome laughter has great face value."

HOW OLD ARE YOU

Children touring a retirement home were asked by a resident if they had any questions. "Yes," answered one girl, "how old are you?"

"I'm 90," she replied proudly!

Clearly impressed the child's eyes grew wide with wonder. "Did you start at one?"

"I've gotten to the age where I need my false teeth and my hearing aid before I can ask where I left my glasses."

HOW DO I STAND

After a thorough physical examination by his doctor, an elderly gent asked, "How do I stand, Doc?"

"That's what puzzles me, too," replied the doctor.

OLD AS THE HILLS

The census taker knocked on the lady's door. She answered all his questions except one. She refused to tell him her age.

"But everyone tells their age to the census taker," he said.

"Did Miss Maisy Hill and Miss Daisy Hill tell you their ages?" she asked.

"Yes they did," he replied.

"Well, I'm the same age as they are," she snapped.

The census taker simply wrote on the form, "As old as the Hills."

"Wrinkles should merely show where smiles have been."
- Mark Twain

SEVEN STAGES OF MAN

Spills – Drills – Thrills – Bills – Ills – Pills – Wills

"Once you're over the hill, you pick up speed."

**"It is only natural for older people to be quiet.
They have a lot more to be quiet about."**

CAN'T GO OUT ANYMORE

Wendell P. Loveless, a writer of sacred music, and associated for many years with Moody Bible Institute Radio Station WMBI, Chicago, said at age 90, "I don't go out much now because my parents won't let me – Mother Nature and Father Time."

SIXTY YEARS AGO

He placed upon your finger a ring of shining gold,
The symbol of your union and love that ne'er grew cold;
Still burns the flame you kindled with brighter purer glow,
Still lives the truth you plighted, just sixty years ago.

The voice that breathed o'er Eden that first sweet wedding day,
Speaks still a benediction on all your pilgrim way;
Has sweetened every sorrow, has blessed in every woe,
For God was in that union, just sixty years ago.

Now hand in hand together, you face the golden nest,
Hope whispers still in gladness, the latter days are best.
With all your children round you, contented onward go,
Your trust in Him who made you, are just sixty years ago.

**"Old folks are worth a fortune, with silver in their hair,
gold in their teeth, stones in their kidneys, lead in their feet,
and gas in their stomachs."**

WHEN YOU GET OLDER

- You don't know real embarrassment until your hip sets off a metal detector.
- You know you're past your prime when every time you suck in your gut, your ankles swell.
- You don't like to do things now that you did twenty years ago – like look in a mirror.
- Your age always corresponds inversely to the size of your multi-vitamin.
- You sit around and watch the sunset, if you can stay up that late.
- You stop looking forward to your next birthday.

**"An old-timer is the married man who can remember when the
only guided missiles were small vases and rolling pins."**

WE'RE NOT GETTING OLDER – JUST MORE MATURE

Today at the drugstore the clerk was a gent
From my purchase this chap took off ten percent.
I asked for the cause of a lesser amount;
And he answered, "Because of the senior's Discount."

I went to McDonald's for a burger and fries;
And there, once again, got quite a surprise,
The clerk poured some coffee which he handed to me
He said, "For you, seniors, the coffee is free."

Understand, I'm not old, I'm merely mature
But some things are changing, temporarily, I'm sure;
The newspaper print gets smaller each day,
And people speak softer, can't hear what they say.

My teeth are my own, I have the receipt,
And my glasses identify people I meet,
Oh, I've slowed down a bit, not a lot, I am sure,
You see, I'm not old, I'm only mature.

The gold in my hair has been bleached by the sun,
You should see all the damage that chlorine has done
Washing my hair has turned it all white
But don't call it grey, saying "blonde" is just right.

My friends all get older, much faster than me
They seem much more wrinkled, from what I can see,
I've got "character lines," not wrinkles, for sure
But don't call me old, just call me mature.

The steps in the houses they're building today
Are so high that they take your breath all away,
And the streets are much steeper than ten years ago,
That should explain why my walking is slow.

But I'm keeping up on what's hip and what's new,
And I think I can still dance a mean boogaloo
I'm still in the running in this I'm secure,
I'm not really old, I'M ONLY MATURE!

"Praise does wonders for the sense of hearing."

"How we leave the world is more important than how we enter it." - Janette Oke

LIFE'S PROGRESS

Ages 1 – 21	Doing what somebody tells you to.
Ages 21 – 65	Doing what you have to.
Ages 65 and up	Doing what you want to.

BIRTHDAY / ANNIVERSARY CARD

An elderly gent entered a stationery store and asked the clerk for a birthday anniversary card. The clerk replied, "We have birthday cards and we have anniversary cards. Why not take one of each?"

The man said, "You don't understand. I need a card that covers 'both' events! You see, we're celebrating the fiftieth anniversary of my wife's thirty-ninth birthday."

"A bald head is at least neat. There are only so many perfect heads; the rest are covered with hair."

OLD AT ANY AGE

You may be old at 40 and young at 80; but you are genuinely old at any age if:

- You feel old.
- You feel that you have learned all there is to learn.
- You find yourself saying, "I'm too old to do that."
- You feel tomorrow holds no promise.
- You take no interest in the activities of youth.
- You would rather talk than listen.
- You long for the 'good old days,' feeling that they were the best.

"To avoid old age, keep taking on new thoughts and throwing off old habits."

HIS FORMULA FOR LIVING

Asked for his formula for long life, Dr. Arthur Judson Brown, Presbyterian minister celebrating his 103rd birthday, quipped, "Don't die!"

"Do you ever stop to think and can't get started again?"

I REMEMBER I'M SEVENTY

My back goes out more than I do,
I sometimes sit to tie up a shoe,
I occasionally forget just who is who,
It is then I remember – I'm seventy!

I take pills and powder to help stay fit,
And exercises I would like to quit,
There are a few more times when I like to sit,
It is then I remember – I'm seventy!

I don't run a race but can walk three miles,
I may sometimes frown, but can still share smiles,
I like my home, not much for the wilds,
It is then I remember – I'm seventy!

God has been good and given me health,
It's not all bad, I tell myself,
I'm not finished yet or on the shelf,
It is then I remember – I'm seventy!

"So teach me to number my days," said He
The One who came and died for me,
Life is so brief compared to eternity,
It is then I remember – I'm seventy!
- A. Daniel Goldsmith

"Growing old is not mandatory; growing up is optional."

I AM NOT A LITTLE WOMAN

I am not a little woman with false dentures and grey hair;
The woman is a little house – I am me, and I live there.
I am not afflicted with a list of symptoms sad and long;
They can only touch my body; I myself am well and strong.
I am not a slave, held helpless by a thousand thongs or things
Clothes and customs and traditions; they bind others – I have wings!
If a brief obituary you should read in the columns of this town
Friend, do not worry, merely say, "Her house fell down."
She herself, escaped uninjured, she has wings, and she can fly,
Look up! See that white bird soaring, on beyond that gull – go I!

"A man is not old until regrets take the place of dreams."

"One nice thing about growing older is that you and your children eventually wind up on the same side of the generation gap." - Barbara Johnson

OLD AGE REVEALS

It isn't easy growing old, but now I know it's true,
Old age reveals what youth conceals, of strength to see you through.
God's bright designs blend beautifully as they through life have done,
And through the dark days God guides us when dark clouds conceal the sun.
It isn't easy growing old, but faith and hope up-springing,
Have made these years, of all years, best – and days of joyful singing.

"After a certain age, if you don't wake up aching in every joint, you are probably dead."

OLD GEEZERS ARE EASY TO SPOT

➢ At sporting events, during the playing of the National Anthem, Old Geezers hold their caps over their hearts and sing without embarrassment. They know the words and believe in them. Old Geezers remember World War I, the Great Depression, World War II, Pearl Harbor, Guadalcanal, Normandy and Hitler.

➢ They remember the Atomic Age, the Korean War, the Cold War, the Jet Age and the Moon Landing, not to mention Vietnam.

➢ If you bump into an Old Geezer on the sidewalk, he will apologize. If you pass an Old Geezer on the street, he will nod or tip his cap to a lady. Old Geezers trust strangers and are courtly to women. Old Geezers hold the door for the next person and always, when walking, make certain the lady is on the inside for protection.

➢ Old Geezers get embarrassed if someone curses in front of women and children and they don't like violence and filth on TV or in movies. Old Geezers have moral courage. They seldom brag unless it's about their grandchildren.

➢ It's the Old Geezers who know our great country is protected not by politicians or police, but by young men and women in the military serving their country. This country needs Old Geezers with their decent values. We need them more than ever.

➢ Thank God for Old Geezers!

"Some people grow old and spread cheer; others just grow old and spread."

"Our five senses are incomplete without the sixth – sense of humor."

HE DOESN'T LOOK AT ME

Amy and Janie are old friends. They have both been married to their husbands for a long time. Amy is upset because she thinks her husband doesn't find her attractive anymore.

"As I get older he doesn't bother to look at me!" Amy cries.

"I'm so sorry for you, as I get older my husband says I get more beautiful every day." replies Janie.

"Yes, but your husband's an antique dealer!"

"We make a living by what we get, but we make a life by what we give." - Sir Winston Churchill

HELPING HIS SON

Harry had worked in construction, but now was retired. His son was building his own home and since Harry was an excellent brick layer, he thought that he would finish off the chimney. Bill, his son, did not have all the latest equipment to work with, it cost too much. So Harry rigged up a beam with a pulley and hoisted up several barrels of bricks.

When he had completed the chimney there were several bricks left over. So he went down the ladder, and began releasing the line. Unfortunately, the barrel of bricks left over was much heavier than he was and before he knew what was happening the barrel started coming down jerking him up. He decided to hang on since he was too far off of the ground to jump.

Half way up he met the barrel of bricks coming down fast. He received a hard blow on his shoulder. He continued to the top, banging his head against the beam and getting his fingers pinched and jammed against the pulley.

When the barrel hit the ground hard it burst its bottom allowing the bricks to spill out. Harry was now heavier than the barrel so he started coming down again at high speed. Half way down he met the barrel going up and received severe injuries to his shins. When he hit the ground he landed on the pile of bricks getting several painful cuts and bruises.

At this point he lost his grip on the line and the barrel came down fast giving him another blow on the head. He ended up in the hospital, enjoying his retirement.

"Old age is when you know your way around, but don't feel like going."

HOW TO KNOW WHEN YOU ARE REALLY, REALLY OLD

When ice-cream cones (even double-headers sometimes) cost only 5 cents.

When milk was only 12 cents a glass quart delivered daily to your door, but you had to leave an empty for the milkman to pick up – also the cream rose to the top of the bottle.

When bread was often delivered fresh daily too, at 10 cents a loaf and for either milk or bread you left the money for it on the front porch.

When a bottle of Pepsi was twice as big as a bottle of Coke, but for the same price. Remember the jingle? "Pepsi Cola hits the spot, drink it when you're cold or hot; biggest drink for a nickel too: Pepsi Cola is the drink for you!"

When those small, sweet, individually wrapped Japanese oranges in their little wooden boxes, which were such a treat, were only available at Christmas time.

When celery was thin and stringy and peaches often had so much fuzz on them you wanted to peel them before you ate them.

When the local butcher shop, with its sawdust strewn floor, was the coolest place in town because every time they opened the door to their walk-in ice box it let cold air into the shop.

When if your shoelace broke you tied a knot in it and used it over again – sometimes ending up with two or three knots before you dared to ask your Mom to buy you new ones.

When worn out shoes were not chucked but rejuvenated by having a shoemaker repair them by nailing or sewing on half-soles.

When driving a car meant learning how to clutch and use a stick-shift. Your "turn signal" was your left arm stuck out the open window, and you dimmed your headlights by pressing a button on the floor with your left foot.

When you didn't discard socks that had holes in but your mother "darned" the holes shut and also sewed patches over the holes in the knees of your denim GWG's and over the hole in the elbow of your plaid shirt.

When you rarely locked your front door and never locked your car.

When it cost 15 cents to go to the Saturday matinee and watch the black and white silent movies accompanied by mood music played on the theatre organ, and the "hook" to come back the following Saturday was to see the next episode of the serial thriller, "The Perils of Pauline."

When the first "talkies" and then first "Technicolor" movies came to your hometown theatre and when you saw the debut of "Gone With The Wind" with Clark Gable and Vivian Leigh and experienced the shock of the first four letter word ever said on the big screen – "damn."
Listening with bated breath as the radio announcer intoned, "Who knows what evil lurks in the minds of men? "The Shadow Knows!" followed by the ominous sounds of impending doom, or waiting in anticipation for the next exciting episode of "The Lone Ranger."

When you could hardly wait for the arrival of the *FAMILY HERALD AND WEEKLY STAR* or the *WESTERN PRODUCER* so you could catch up on the adventures of "Buck Rogers", "Prince Valiant", "Little Orphan Annie" or "Little Annie Rooney" and laugh at "Maggie and Jiggs", "Mutt and Jeff", "Blondie", "Lil' Abner" and "The Flintstones".

Turning in to "Hockey Night in Canada" on the radio with the exciting play by play announcing of Foster Hewitt with his trademark saying, "He shoots! He scores!"

When the National Hockey League had only six teams, two from Canada and four from the USA. Can you name them?

When your Mom and/or you, used to tune in on radio's early "soaps" – "One Man's Family" or "Ma Perkins."

When if you got the strap at school you'd probably get a licking to match it when you arrived home.

When gentlemen always walked on the street side of the sidewalk when walking with a lady and never ever swore in a lady's presence.

When young people (we didn't have any teen-agers back then) were not ashamed to be picked up at school by their parents.

When the usual breakfast fare was porridge (oatmeal, cream of wheat or sometimes Red River Cereal) and you longed for summer to come when your Mom would finally give in to your begging and buy cold cereals, which cost a lot more.

When there were NO sweetened cereals, just plain corn flakes, bran flakes, puffed wheat, puffed rice, rice krispies and shredded wheat, and of course Jack Armstrong's "The all American boy's" Wheaties – "The best breakfast food in the land!" the jingle said.

When as a kid at the table, you ate what was served you, no complaints, no substitutes, there was nothing else! [4] - Bert Warden

"What a married couple should save for their old age are each other."

"Take time to laugh, it is the music of the soul."

GRANDPA'S A NUT

Herman A. Conn, my father-in-law, died at the hospital June 7, 1983 at the age of 85. Our 7 year old son, David, was present and he could not understand how Grandpa, having just passed away, could still be lying there and also be in Heaven. I tried to explain what happens when a Christian dies, but the terms used only confused him. Finally he said, "Mom forget it." I told Grandma what he had said.

Later David again asked why Grandpa's body was still there the day of the funeral, and this time Grandma did the explaining. She told him about the walnut, how we open the outer shell and eat what is inside, which is the best part. Then we toss away the shell. "That's what happened to Grandpa," she said. "God left the old, outer shell on earth and took the best part of Grandpa to Heaven – the inside, his soul." This completely satisfied our 7 year old's curiosity about why Grandpa could be in Heaven even though we could still see his body.

Later that day, as my son came running down the stairs, he said to me "Grandpa was a nut." I wondered why he made such a statement until I talked with Grandma and learned of the explanation she had given him.

It isn't easy to teach our children about death. I think Grandma's illustration was priceless.
- Sharon Conn

"In youth we run into difficulties; in old age difficulties run into us."

PLAIN ENGLISH

A man recently retired and realized that he was no longer motivated to do any work around the house, or anywhere. His wife suggested that he go see his doctor. After sharing with the doctor how he felt and that he lacked any kind of motivation, he said to the doctor, "Please give it to me in plain English. I can never understand or remember all those medical terms."

"Well, in plain English," said the doctor, "you're simply just plain lazy."

"Okay," said the man, "now will you give me the medical term so I can tell my wife."

CHILDHOOD

I worked in a nursing home and each new resident was interviewed by a social worker. A happy looking 96 year old man was asked, "Did you have a happy childhood?"

"So far so good," he replied.

**"Some people cause happiness wherever they go,
others whenever they go."**

SO OLD

- He remembers when the big dipper was a drinking cup.
- At his birthday party the guests were overcome with the heat of the candles.
- He feels like the Liberty Bell – old, heavy, and slightly cracked.
- When he was born the Dead Sea was only sick.

FEARFULLY AND WONDERFULLY MADE

Since I have reached this middle age,
No more a youth, but now a sage;
I've found it takes both hook and tether
To hold my body all together.
For when I go to bed at night,
Before I pray and out the light,
I doff my shoes, remove my socks,
Wind the cat, put out the clocks,
Then lay the hair from off my head
Upon the stand beside my bed.
Take off my glasses, out my teeth
Placed beside my watch and key,
Remove my aid, my hearing's dim
Un-do the hooks to wooden limb;
Take lashes, false, from off my eyes
And fall in bed with weary sighs.
Oh, isn't growing old just grand!
Two-thirds of me are on the stand!
But husband loves me, he just said,
He means the third that's in his bed.

THIRTY-NINE AND HOLDING

A young child asked an older woman how old she was. The woman answered, "39 and holding."

The child thought for a moment, then asked, "How old would you be if you let go?"

**"In my day, we couldn't afford shoes, so we went barefoot.
In the winter we had to wrap our feet with
barbed wire for traction."** - Bill Flavin

SEVEN AGES OF MAN

Six weeks – all systems go
Six years – all systems "No!"
Sixteen years – all systems know.
Twenty-six years – all systems glow.
Thirty-six years – all systems owe.
Fifty-six years – all systems status quo.
Seventy-six years – all systems slow.

"By the time you're eighty years old you've learned everything. You only have to remember it." - George Burns

I AM MY OWN GRANDFATHER

A psychiatrist was visiting in a ward in a California hospital and asked a patient: "How did you get here? What was the nature of your illness?"

The patient replied and said: "Well, it all started when I got married and I guess I should never have done it. I married a widow with a grown daughter who then became my step-daughter. My dad came to visit us and fell in love with my lovely step-daughter and married her. And so my step-daughter was now my stepmother. Soon, my wife had a son who was, of course, my daddy's brother-in-law since he is the half-brother of my step-daughter, who is now, of course, my daddy's wife. So, as I told you, when my step-daughter married my daddy, she was at once my stepmother! Now, since my new son is brother to my step-mother, he also became my uncle. As you know, my wife is my step-grandmother since she is my step-mother's mother. Don't forget that my step-mother is my step-daughter. Remember, too, that I am my wife's grandson. But hold on just a few minutes more. You see, since I'm married to my step-grandmother, I am not only the wife's grandson and her hubby, but I am also my own grandfather. Now can you understand how I got put in this place?"

"We spent our youth trying to obtain wealth, and now we spend our wealth trying to obtain youth."

ARE YOU HIRING

An elderly lady walked up to the manager of a department store and asked: "Are you hiring any help?"

"No," he said. "We have all the staff that we need."

"Then would you mind getting someone to wait on me?" she asked.

CHEWING GUM WHILE FLYING

Grandma Esther was taking her very first flight. She was traveling from Montreal to Miami. The aircraft had only been aloft a few minutes when the elderly lady complained to the flight attendant that her ears were popping.

The flight attendant smiled and gave the older woman some chewing gum, assuring her that many people experienced the same discomfort and that gum was good for the ears.

When they landed in Miami, Grandma thanked the flight attendant. "The chewing gum worked fine," she said, "but tell me, how do I get it out of my ears."

"I am wondering, if you are only as old as you feel, how could I be alive at 150?"

A MORNING PRAYER

"Dear Lord, so far today, I am doing all right. I have not gossiped, lost my temper, been greedy, grumpy, nasty, selfish, or self-indulgent. I have not whined, complained, or eaten any chocolate. I have charged nothing on my credit card. But I will be getting out of bed in a minute, and I think that I will really need Your help then."

SCHOOL DAYS

Reminiscing about his school days, a gentleman said, "The school that I attended turned out some great men."

"When did you graduate?" his friend asked.

"I didn't graduate. I was one that was turned out."

"Tomorrow's memories come from today's decisions."

CAN I CLIMB THE STAIRS NOW?

An old lady who lived on the second floor of a rooming house was warned by the doctor, as he placed a cast on her broken leg, not to climb stairs. After several weeks he took off the cast.

"Can I climb stairs now?" she asked.

"Yes," the doctor replied.

"Good. I'm sick and tired of shinnying up and down that drainpipe!"

"He's so old he doesn't learn history, he remembers it."

FOUR STAGES OF MAN

- When you believe in Santa Claus
- When you don't believe in Santa Claus
- When you are Santa Claus
- When you look like Santa Claus

RICH INDEED

A tax collector one day came to a poor pastor in order to assess the value of his property and to determine the amount of his taxes.

"I am a rich man," said the pastor.

The official quickly sharpened his pencil and asked intently, "Well, what do you own?"

"I am the possessor of a Savior who earned for me everlasting life and who has prepared a place for me in the Eternal City."

"What else?"

"I have a brave, pious wife, and the Bible says, 'Who can find a virtuous woman? For her price is far above rubies'."

"What else?"

"Healthy and obedient children."

"What else?"

"A merry heart which enables me to pass through life joyfully."

"What else?"

"That is all," replied the pastor.

The official closed his book, arose, took his hat and said, "You are indeed a rich man, sir, but your property is not subject to taxation." - George Henderson

"As a senior, don't try to keep up with the freshmen class."

"Money has been defined as a universal provider of everything but happiness, and a passport to everywhere but Heaven."

SECRET TO A SUCCESSFUL MARRIAGE

When Mr. & Mrs. Henry Ford celebrated their golden wedding anniversary, a reporter asked them, "To what do you attribute your fifty years of successful married life?"

Henry Ford responded by saying, "The formula is the same one I've used in making cars, just stick to one model."

KEEP IT SECRET

A pastor announced that admission to a church social event would be $6.00 per person. "However, if you're over 65," he said, "the price will be only $5.50."

From the back of the congregation a woman's voice rang out, "Do you really think I'd give you that information for only 50 cents?"

"When a woman laughs at her husband's jokes, either they're good jokes, or she's a good wife."

LOOKING GOOD

Soon after our last child left home for college, my husband was resting next to me on the couch with his head in my lap. I carefully removed his glasses. "You know, honey," I said sweetly, "without your glasses you look like the same handsome young man I married."

"Honey," he replied, "without my glasses, you still look pretty good too!"

DANGEROUS CRIMINAL

One autumn night, an older lady, with a black eye, stumbled into the police station. She told the police that she heard a noise in her back yard and went to investigate. She told the police that she was struck in the eye and was knocked out cold.

An officer was sent to her house to investigate. About an hour and a half later, he returned and he also had a black eye.

"Did you get hit by the same person?" the captain asked.

"No," he replied, "I stepped on the same rake."

"If the most exercise you get in a day is crawling out of bed, you could double your exercise by crawling back into bed."

THE METRIC SYSTEM

An old timer tried to imagine what the metric system would do to some of our proverbs. Imagine:
- ❖ "A kilogram of flesh."
- ❖ "A 30.48 centimeter-long hot dog."
- ❖ "A miss is as good as 1,609 kilometers."
- ❖ "It hit me like 907 kilograms of bricks."
- ❖ "Peter Piper picked 8.81 liters of pickled peppers."
- ❖ "Give him 2.54 centimeters and he'll take 1,609 kilometers."
- ❖ "28.350 grams of prevention are worth 453.592 grams of cure."

"It's hard to be nostalgic when you can't remember anything."

SASKATCHEWAN vs TEXAS

A Saskatchewan farmer had just finished showing his friend from Texas around his six sections (3,840 acres), which took three to four hours just to walk around the boundaries.

As the tour had finished and they were approaching the farm house, the Texan said, "You should come and see my ranch – its' BIG! Why it takes me two full days to drive around it."

"I understand perfectly," said his host. "I once owned a truck like that."

"In the good old days, you paddled your own canoe, but now an outboard motor does it for you."

HE WAS A SAINT

Mrs. James offered the minister a large donation to the church if, at her husband's funeral, he'd say that the man had been a saint. "Your husband lied, cheated and stole," answered the minister. "I could never say he was a saint!"

"Then I'll ruin your reputation," she threatened.

Fearing for his job, the minister began the service with these words, "Mr. James was a liar, a cheat and a thief… but compared to his wife, he was a saint."

"A chuckle a day may not keep the doctor away, but it sure does make those times in life's waiting room a little more bearable."
- Ann Schaef

"You can't turn back the clock, but you can wind it up again."

GO RIGHT AHEAD WITH YOUR KNITTIN'

When the folks next to you act like those in the zoo,
    A grumblin', a growlin' and spittin',
It's a pretty good plan to be calm as you can,
    And do somethin' useful – like knittin'.

When a gossipin' Susan, with poison-barbed tongue,
    Comes into the room where you're sittin'
And starts to defame some neighbor's good name,
    Count stitches out loud – and keep knittin'.

When there's been a slight misunderstanding at church,
    And others hint broadly of quittin',
Why, the very best thing you can do is to sing
    And stay at your post – and keep knittin'.

When Satan moves in with his cohorts of sin,
    Say, You'll never find me submittin',
You irk me, I find, so get thee behind
    And please don't disturb me – I'm knittin'.

In the middle of problems, the big ones and small
    It's always most proper and fittin'
To trust and to pray till the Lord shows the way
    And go right ahead with your knittin'.

**"Oh, God, keep me from becoming a foolish old man.
Help me end well."** - Dr. Harry A. Ironside

COUNT YOUR BLESSINGS

Count your blessings instead of your crosses,
Count your gains instead of your losses.
Count your joys instead of your woes
Count your friends instead of your foes.
Count your smiles instead of your tears
Count your courage instead of your fears.
Count your full years instead of your lean
Count your kind deeds instead of your mean.
Count your health instead of your wealth
Count on God instead of yourself.

"When a man dies, if he can pass enthusiasm along to his children he has left them an estate of incalculable value." - Thomas Edison

OLD AGE BEGINS

In a seminar for senior citizens, a person asked a geriatrics specialist, "When do the signs of old age begin?"

The doctor thought for a moment and then answered, "At conception."

JUST CHECKING

An elderly woman, calling a local hospital, said, "Hello, I'd like to talk with the person who gives the information regarding your patients. I'd like to find out if the patient is getting better, or doing as expected, or is getting worse."

The voice on the other end of the line said, "What is the patient's name and room number?"

The woman replied, "Sarah Finkel, in room 302."

"I will connect you with the nursing station"

"3-A Nursing Station. How can I help you?"

"I would like to know the condition of Sarah Finkel in room 302."

"Just a moment. Let me look at her records. Oh, yes, Mrs. Finkel is doing very well. In fact, she's had two full meals, her blood pressure is fine, her blood work just came back as normal, she's going to be taken off the heart monitor in a couple of hours and if she continues this improvement, Dr. Cohen is going to send her home Tuesday at twelve o'clock."

The woman said, "Thank God! That's wonderful! Oh that's fantastic! That's wonderful news!"

The nurse said, "From your enthusiasm, I take it you must be a close family member or a very close friend!"

"Not exactly, I'm Sarah Finkel in 302. Nobody here tells me anything!"

NEED SOMETHING OLD

Old shoes are easiest, and old friends are best. We are used to them; they fit us and we cannot bear to part with them. Bring me my old slippers when my feet ache, and fetch me my old friends when my heart aches." - Dr. Vance Havner

"Remember the old days when people killed time by working instead of by coffee breaks."

REMEMBER JIMMY DURANTE

"I goes into the automat and puts a lead nickel in da slot. And what do you think comes out? The manager!"

"I'm lyin' on the park bench takin' my siesta, as is my wont, when along comes a bunch of flies and settle on my nose. I lets 'em loiter. Live and let live is my motter. Den a bee comes along, lights on my nose and stings me. Dat does it!" I says, "Dere's always gotta be smart aleck in every crowd. Now, just for that, everybody off."

"A guy tells me, 'Hey, Jimmy, there's a fly on the end of your nose. Why don't you brush it off?' I tells him, "it's closer to you dan it is ta me."

"When I was a young man, no one had any respect for youth. Now I am an old man and no one has any respect for age." - B. Russell

LITTLE PILL, WHERE GOEST THOU?

We take pink pills for old arthritis, and green ones, perhaps, for the heart.
A blue one because you are dizzy, hope the stomach can tell them apart.
A white pill controls the blood pressure, a red one helps soften the stool;
A yellow one calms you down greatly, so you won't be acting the fool.
There are two-toned, and gray and brown pills, for relief from head-aches and gout,
Diabetes, ulcers and heartburn, sure hope each pill knows the right route.
What a terrible mess up there could be, if your headache pill went to your toe,
And the laxative pill traveled upward, 'cause it wasn't quite sure where to go.
If this should ever happen to you, you'd either laugh or you'd weep.
'Cause you'd probably run off at the mouth, and your feet would be falling asleep.
How in the world could you stop the dilemma, unless you stood on your head?
So the pills could all change directions, before you wound up sick in bed.
What would happen if time released capsules forgot to do the right thing
And released all their pellets at once, a great upset they would bring.
So little pills of every kind, just wend your way thru us and find
The ailment that we take you for, so we won't worry anymore!
- Ester Stout

"The kind of successor I may get may depend a great deal on the kind of predecessor I've been and how I've related to my own predecessor." - Dr. Warren Wiersbe

LEFT WITH THE GOSPEL

Dr. Baldwin, who was pastor of a church for forty-nine years, said:

"I testify that at thirty, after examining as best I could the philosophies and religions of the world, I said, 'Nothing is better than the Gospel of Christ.'

At forty, when burdens began to press heavily and years seemed to hasten, I said, 'Nothing is as good as the Gospel.'

At fifty, when there were empty chairs in the home, and the mound builders had done me service, I said, 'There is nothing to be compared with the Gospel.'

At sixty, when my second sight saw through the delusions and vanities of earthly things, I said, 'There is nothing but the Gospel.'

At seventy, amid many limitations and deprivations, I sing:
> *Should all the forms that men devise*
> *Attack my faith with treacherous art,*
> *I'd call them vanities and lies*
> *And bind the Gospel to my heart."*

"An aged Christian with the snow of time upon his head reminds us that those points of earth are the whitest which are nearest to Heaven."

THE GOLDEN YEARS

Old age is golden I've oft heard it said,
But I hardly can believe it when I go to bed.
I put my ears in a drawer, my teeth in a cup,
My glasses on the table until time to get up.
And before sleep seals my eyelids, I say to myself,
"Is there anything else I must put on the shelf?"

But then comes the answer, "You still have a soul;
The spirit within you is gloriously whole
And forever will shine in the City of Light."
Yes, old age is golden because 'twill bring us one day
To joy everlasting, to peace evermore
With the Father of Light on the Eternal Shore.
- Nellie Beach

"Many a retired husband becomes his wife's full-time job."

LIKE MOTHER USED TO MAKE

I can sing and I can play,
I can sew the livelong day,
   And I always thought that I could first-rate bake.
Be it bread or cake or pie,
I can hear his soft reply,
   "It is good, but not like Mother used to make."

Now at first it broke my heart,
For to cook is quite an art,
   Which I thought I had accomplished – a mistake!
But I don't grieve anymore,
Laugh instead of getting "sore"
   When I hear, "It's not like Mother used to make."

For I think I've won at last
In the future, not the past,
   For I have six boys who sometime wives will take.
Be it bread or cake or pie,
I can hear the soft reply,
   "It is good, but not like Mother used to make."
                - Helen Hale

50th ANNIVERSARY DINNER

Grand pappy and his wife were discussing their 50th wedding anniversary, when she said, "Shall I kill a chicken tonight?"

"Naw," said Grand pappy. "Why blame a bird for something that happened 50 years ago?"

MIDDLE AGE

The years are creeping up on you
When you are moved to deplore…
That awful morning-after feeling
Without the night before!!!

"We arrived in this world with no luggage and no material possessions. We leave the same way."

**"More people would live to a ripe old age if
they weren't too busy providing for it."**

HOW MANY DO YOU REMEMBER

Blackjack chewing gum   Candy cigarettes
Brownie cameras   Peashooters
Sleigh bells on horses' harnesses   78 rpm records
View Master   Blue flashbulbs
Ration cards   Black & White TV
Roller skate keys   Cork popguns
Wash-tub ringers   Studebakers
Ink wells in school desks   Gestetner stencils
Metal ice-cube trays with lever   Howdy Doody
Telephone numbers with a word prefix (i.e. Cherry 7455)
Home milk delivery in glass bottles with cardboard stoppers
Restaurants with table-side juke-box controls

"Everyone wants to live long, but no one wants to be called old."
- Icelandic Proverb

GLADYS DUNN

A lady was visiting a church for the very first time. The sermon seemed to go on and on forever, and many in the congregation actually fell asleep.

After the service, endeavoring to be sociable and hoping to meet some new friends, she walked over to a very sleepy looking elderly gentleman, extended her hand in greeting, and said, "Hello, I'm Gladys Dunn."

The elderly gent replied, "You're not the only one ma'am. I'm glad it's done too!"

YOUR AGE PLEASE

"Your age, please?" asked the census taker.

"Well," said the woman, "let me figure it out. I was 18 when I was married and my husband was 30. He is now 60, or twice as old as he was then, so I am now 36."

**"Life really isn't fair. You eat properly, exercise and take good
care of yourself for sixty years, and what's your reward?
Old age!"**

"You stop growing when you stop learning." - Henry Ford

ARTHUR GODFREY

Years ago, I remember listening to Arthur Godfrey do a radio ad for a cure-all medicine. The ad went, "At last, hope for middle age." Godfrey paused and said, "I've got hope. What I need is help." - Fred Smith

GO SLOW

Two older women boarded the airplane at the same time as their pilots. "Now don't go faster than sound," said one of the women to the pilots, "we want to talk."

"In the good old days we were broke and lived on hamburger. Now we live on hamburger and we are broke."

CONTEST WINNERS

A couple we know recently attended their 60 year high school class reunion. During the evening they were chosen to head a group that would judge the Old Smoothies dance contest. The husband has a hearing problem and his wife has been trying to get him to get a hearing aid. When the contest got down to the last two partners, the wife conferred with the group of judges and then whispered the name of the winners to her husband. He didn't hear, so she told him again and then yelled, "Get the bananas out of your ears!"

The husband immediately seized the microphone and announced that the winners were "Mr. and Mrs. Bonnanas!" Their name turned out to be Smith. That wasn't bad enough. The wife then explained to the Smiths that they had won because they did such a great job of executing all those dips.

"Dips? What dips?" said Mr. Smith. "We were just trying to hold each other up."

"Aging has the ability to change an attractive young chick into a gracious old hen." - A. Daniel Goldsmith

HIS PHILOSOPHY WASN'T GOOD

An old fellow was sitting enjoying the shade of a big old walnut tree wondering why God had placed a large pumpkin on a small vine and a little walnut on a large tree. While he was philosophizing, a walnut fell from the tree and hit the man on the head. He rubbed his head ruefully and said, "I'm thankful that God did not put pumpkins on that tree."

"By the time you can make ends meet, they move the ends."

"The best way to tell a woman's age is in a whisper."

A MOTHER AT 65

A lady of 65 had a baby which shook the medical fraternity. When she arrived home, the press were waiting for her. After a short interview, the press asked to see the baby. "In a few minutes," she said.

Half hour later the press asked again to see the baby and got the same answer, "In a few minutes."

An hour later the press asked why they could not see the baby. The lady replied, "You will have to wait until the baby cries."

"Why should we have to wait until the baby cries?" asked the press.

"I have forgotten where I put the baby," replied the 65 year old mother.

"Middle age is the time of life when work begins to be a lot less fun and fun begins to be a lot more work."

GARDENING MADE EASY

An elderly man who lived alone in Ireland wanted to spade his garden so that he could plant his potatoes. It was too hard a job for him. His only son, who would have helped him, was in Long Kesh Prison. So the elderly man wrote a letter to his son and mentioned his predicament.

Shortly, he received a letter from his son. "Dad, don't dig up that garden. That's where I buried the guns!"

At 4:00am the next morning, a dozen British soldiers showed up and dug the entire garden, without finding any guns.

Confused, the old man wrote another note to his son telling him what had happened, and asking him what to do next.

His son's reply was: "Now plant your potatoes, Dad. It's the best I could do at this time."

LOVED TO TRAVEL

At age 20 I could hardly wait for vacation so that I could "hit the road" and travel. By the time I was 35 I had been practicing for years how to go from 0 to 60 miles per hour in eight seconds. At the age of 50, I found that I had been holding the map upside down. At 70, I discovered that I had the wrong map.

"If you don't learn to laugh at trouble, you won't have anything to laugh at when you are old."

ADVICE FROM A DIETITIAN

A dietitian was once addressing a large audience in Chicago. "The material we put into our stomachs is enough to have killed most of us sitting here, years ago. Red meat is awful. Soft drinks erode your stomach lining. Chinese food is loaded with MSG, and none of us realizes the long-term harm caused by the germs in our drinking water.

But there is one thing that is most dangerous of all and we all have, or will eat it. Can anyone here tell me what food it is that causes the most grief and suffering for years after eating it?"

A 75-year old man in the front row stood up and said, "Wedding cake!"

A DRUG PROBLEM

Melvin Graham, Billy Graham's brother, shared the following at one of Dr. Graham's crusades: I had a "drug" problem when I was a young person and teenager.

I was "drug" to church on Sunday morning.
I was "drug" to church on Sunday night.
I was "drug" to church on Wednesday night.
I was "drug" to Sunday School ever week.
I was "drug" to Vacation Bible School.
I was "drug" to the family altar to read the Bible and pray.
I was also "drug" to the woodshed when I disobeyed my parents.

Those "drugs" are still in my veins, and they affect my behavior in everything I do, say, and think. They are stronger than cocaine, crack or heroin, and if our children had this kind of "drug" problem, America and Canada would certainly be a better place.

"Growing old is not upsetting; being perceived as old is." - K. Rogers

A WALKING ECONOMY

Two retirees were out walking in the park. One of them said to his friend, "I'm a walking economy."

The friend asked, "How is that?"

"Well," said the retiree, "my hair line is in recession, my stomach is a victim of inflation, and both of these together are putting me into a deep depression!"

47

GRANDMA'S DIARY

When Grandma was married and learning to cook, she started keeping a diary. Here is a week out of her new bride's diary.

Monday: It's fun to cook for Bob. Today I made angel food cake. The recipe said beat 12 eggs separately. The neighbors were nice enough to loan me some extra bowls.

Tuesday: Bob wanted fruit salad for supper. The recipe said serve without dressing. So I didn't dress.

Wednesday: A good day for rice. The recipe said wash thoroughly before steaming the rice. It seemed kinda silly but I took a bath. I can't say it improved the rice any.

Thursday: Today Bob asked for salad again. I tried a new recipe. It said prepare ingredients, then toss on a bed of lettuce an hour before serving, which is what led up to Bob asking me why I was rolling around in the garden.

Friday: I found an easy recipe for cookies. It said put all the ingredients in a bowl and beat it. There must have been something wrong with this recipe. When I got back, everything was the same as when I left.

Saturday: Bob did the shopping today and brought home a chicken. He asked me to dress it for Sunday (oh boy). For some reason Bob keeps counting to ten.

Sunday: Bob's folks came to dinner. I wanted to serve roast. All I could find was hamburger. Suddenly I had a flash of genius. I put hamburger in the oven and set the controls to roast. It still came out hamburger, much to my disappointment.

Good night dear diary. This has been a very exciting week. I am eager for tomorrow to come so I can try out a new recipe on Bob. If we could just get a bigger oven, I would like to surprise him with Chocolate Moose.

I AM OLD FASHIONED ENOUGH

To believe that a certain amount of work is good for any child.
To think that most men want to do the right thing.
To remember that the Sabbath day was meant to be kept holy.
To insist upon women holding modesty in high esteem.
To expect that any law for the good of the people can be enforced.
To vote for the man who does the least talking and gets the biggest results.

"Growing old – it's not nice, but it's interesting." - August Strindberg

"To make success of old age a fellow sure has to start young."

WRITING A PRAISE CHORUS

Grandpa was visiting his young grandson Jordan. Jordan was showing him his new guitar and explaining how he was learning to write contemporary praise choruses.

"Play one of your compositions for me," said Grandpa.

"I'll play the one that I wrote yesterday," said Jordan. "It only has one stanza but you sing it seven times." - A. Daniel Goldsmith

"Old friends are like antiques, they are to be treasured."

BEHIND IN MATH

The newly retired gent was enjoying his coffee break at Starbucks. Across from him was a woman, in her sixties, who was engrossed in her newspaper. One of the headlines blared: "12 Brazilian Soldiers Killed." She shook her head at the sad news.

Then, turning to him she asked, "How many is a Brazilian?"

THEY BOTH CAME BACK

The physician phoned one of his senior patients. "Mrs. Taylor," he said, "I'm sorry to tell you this, but your check just came back."

"So did my arthritis," she replied, and hung up.

"A friend is someone who knows the song in your heart and can sing it back to you when you have forgotten the words."

BREAKABLE

There was this elderly lady who was mailing an old family Bible to her brother in another part of the country. "Is there anything breakable in here?" asked the postal clerk.

"Only the Ten Commandments," answered the lady.

"Man is the only animal that laughs, but when you look at some people, it is hard to understand how the animals keep from laughing."

"An old-timer is one who remembers when a family that couldn't afford to own a car, didn't."

DON'T TOUCH ME

An older couple were lying in bed one morning, having just awakened from a good night's sleep. He took her hand and she said, "Don't touch me."

"Why not?" he asked.

She answered back, "Because I'm dead!"

The husband said, "What are you talking about? We're both lying here in bed together and talking to one another."

She said, "No, I'm definitely dead."

He insisted, "You're not dead. What in the world makes you think you're dead?"

"Because I woke up this morning and nothing hurts."

"They shall still bring forth fruit in old age..." Psalm 92:14

MEANING OF THE BIBLE

A grandfather was approached by his small grandson, who told him proudly, "I know what the Bible means!"

The grandfather smiled and replied, "What do you mean, you 'know' what the Bible means?"

His grandson replied, "I do know!"

"Okay," said his grandfather. "So tell me what does the Bible mean?"

"That's easy, Grandpa. It stands for 'Basic Information Before Leaving Earth'."

LAST WILL & TESTAMENT

An elderly woman decided to prepare her will and told her preacher she had two final requests. First, she wanted to be cremated, and second, she wanted her ashes scattered over at Wal-Mart.

"Wal-Mart?" the preacher exclaimed, "Why Wal-Mart?"

"Then I'll be sure my daughters visit me twice each week."

**"It is so sad that many seniors are like plants.
Some go to seed with age and others go to pot."**

APRONS

I don't think our kids know what an apron is. The principal use of Grandma's apron was to protect the dress underneath, but along with that, it served as a potholder for removing hot pans from the oven. It was wonderful for drying children's tears, and on occasion was even used for cleaning out dirty ears. From the chicken coop, the apron was used for carrying eggs, fussy chicks, and sometimes half-hatched eggs to be finished in the warming oven.

When company came, those aprons were ideal hiding places for shy kids. And when the weather was cold, grandma wrapped it around her arms. Those big old aprons wiped many a perspiring brow, over the hot wood stove. Chips and kindling wood were brought into the kitchen in that apron. From the garden, it carried all sorts of vegetables. After the peas had been shelled, it carried out the hulls.

In the fall, the apron was used to bring in apples that had fallen from the trees. When unexpected company drove up the road, it was surprising how much furniture that old apron could dust in a matter of seconds. When dinner was ready, Grandma walked out onto the porch, waved her apron, and the men knew it was time to come in from the fields to dinner. It will be a long time before someone invents something that will replace that "old-time apron" that served so many purposes.

**"A good wife is one who can see through her husband
and still enjoy the view."**

REMEMBER

Grandma used to set her hot baked apple pies on the window sill to cool.
Her grand-daughters set their apple pies on the window sill to thaw.

HEARING AIDS

An elderly gentleman had serious hearing problems for a number of years. He went to the doctor and the doctor was able to have him fitted for a set of hearing aids that allowed the gentleman to hear 100%.

The gentleman went back in a month to the doctor and the doctor said, "Your hearing is perfect. Your family must be really pleased that you can hear again."

The elderly gent replied, "Oh, I haven't told my family yet. I just sit around and listen to the conversations. I've also changed my will three times!"

JUST CHECKING

During my brother's wedding, my mother managed to keep from crying until she glanced at my grandparents. My grandmother had reached over to my grandfather's wheelchair and gently touched his hand. That was all it took to start my mother's tears flowing.

After the wedding, Mom went over to my grandmother and told her how that tender gesture triggered her outburst.

"Well, I'm sorry to ruin your moment," grandmother replied, "but I was just checking to see if he was still alive."

"Grow old along with me! The best is yet to be, the last of life for which the first was made." - Robert Browning

A SENIOR WITH A GOOD APPETITE

Methuselah ate what he found on his plate
And never as people do now,
Ignoring the amount of the calorie count,
He ate it because it was chow.
With ne'er a debate as at dinner he ate
Devouring a roast or a pie,
Nor thought, as he sat, of granular fat,
Nor if it was vitamin shy.
He always found good every plateful of food
Unmindful of worries and fears,
That his health might be hurt
By some tasty dessert,
And he lived over nine hundred years

HARD OF HEARING

Three retirees, each with a hearing loss, were taking a walk one fine spring day. One of them remarked to the others, "Windy, ain't it?"

"No," one of them remarked. "It's Thursday."

The third man chimed in, "So am I, let's get a Pepsi."

"Every time I think of running, I lie down and it goes away."
- Dr. Howard Hendricks

"I used to watch golf on TV but my doctor told me that I need more exercise, so now I watch tennis."

SENILITY PRAYER

Dear Lord please help me to forget the friends I didn't like in the first place;
help me to bump into the ones I do like;
and please give me the ability to tell the difference.

WALKING AROUND THE BLOCK

Tim and Harry were having coffee at Starbucks. Tim said, "Well I finally realized that I needed to do more exercise so I joined the walking club at the Sevenoaks Mall."

"That's good, but I don't have to go to any mall or track to get my exercise," said Harry. "I started a few days ago by placing a block in the center of the living room. I walk around the block every day."

"Interesting," said Tim.

"Yep," said Harry, "I walked around the block seven times this morning."

"Life is not measured by the number of breaths we take, but by the moments that take our breath away."

MOMENTS

Happy moments, praise God. Difficult moments, seek God.
Quiet moments, worship God. Painful moments, trust God.
Every moment, thank God.

I WAS HER PUMPKIN PIE

Before I married Maggie dear, I was her pumpkin pie,
Her precious peach and honey boy, the apple of her eye,
But after years of married life this thought I pause to utter,
Those fancy names are now all gone; I'm just her bread and butter.

"You are getting older if you remember when popular music made you want to tap your foot on the floor, not bang your head against the wall."

A WALK DOWN MEMORY LANE

A little house with three bedrooms and one car on the street,
A mower that you had to push to make the grass look neat.
In the kitchen on the wall we only had one phone,
And no need for recording things someone was always home.

We only had a living room where we would congregate,
Unless it was at meal time in the kitchen where we ate.
We had no need for family rooms or extra rooms to dine,
When meeting as a family those two rooms would work out fine.

We only had one TV set and channels maybe two,
But always there was one of them with something worth the view.
For snacks we had potato chips that tasted like a chip,
And if you wanted flavor there was Lawson's onion dip.

Store bought snacks were rare because my mother liked to cook,
And nothing can compare to snacks in Betty Crocker's Cookbook.
The snacks were even healthy with the best ingredients,
There was no label with a hundred things that made no sense.

Weekends were for family trips or staying home to play,
We all did things together even go to church to pray.
When we did our weekend trips depending on the weather,
No one stayed at home because we liked to be together.

Sometimes we would separate to do things on our own,
But we knew where the others were without our own cell phone.
Then there were the movies with your favorite movie star,
And nothing can compare to watching movies in your car.

Then there were the picnics at the peak of summer season,
Pack a lunch and find some trees and never need a reason.
Get a baseball game together with the friends you know,
Have real action playing ball and no game video.

Remember when the doctor used to be the family friend,
And didn't need insurance or a lawyer to defend,
The way that he took care of you or what he had to do,
Because he took an oath and strove to do the best for you.

Remember when the country was united under God,
And prayer in schools and public places was not deemed as being odd.
Remember when the church was used for worshipping the Lord,
And not used for commercial use or for some business board.

Remember going to the store and shopping casually,
And when you went to pay for it you used your own money,
Nothing that you had to swipe or punch in some amount,
Remember when the cashier person had to really count?

Remember when we breathed the air it smelled so fresh and clean,
And chemicals were not used on the grass to keep it green.
The milkman and the bread man used to go from door to door,
And it was just a few cents more than going to the store.

There was a time when mailed letters came right to your door,
Without a lot of junk mail ads sent out by every store,
The mailman knew each house by name and knew where it was sent,
There were not loads of mail addressed to present occupant.

Remember when the words "I do" meant that you really did,
And not just temporarily till someone blew their lid,
There was no thing as no one's fault; we just made a mistake.
There was a time when married life was built on give and take.

There was a time when just one glance was all that it would take,
And you would know the kind of car, the model and the make,
They didn't look like turtles trying to squeeze every mile,
They were streamlined, white walls and fins and really had some style.

One time the music that you played when ever you would jive,
Was from a vinyl, big holed record called a forty-five,
The record player had a post to keep them all in line,
And then the records would drop down and play one at a time.

Oh sure we had our problems then just like we do today,
And always we were striving trying for a better way.
And every year that passed us by brought new and greater things,
We now can even program phones with music or with rings.

Oh the simple life we lived still seems like so much fun,
How can you explain a game, just kick the can and run?
And why would boys put baseball cards between bicycle spokes?
And for a nickel red machines had little bottled cokes.

This life seemed so much easier and slower in some ways,
I love the new technology but I sure miss those good old days.
So time moves on and so do we and nothing stays the same,
But I sure love to reminisce and walk down memory lane.

"The quickest way to become an old dog is to stop learning new tricks." - J. Rooney

GRUMPY OLD MAN

While on a road trip, an elderly couple stopped at a roadside restaurant for lunch. After finishing their meal, they left the restaurant and resumed their trip. When leaving, the elderly woman unknowingly left her glasses on the table but she didn't miss them until after they had been driving about twenty minutes. By then, to add to the aggravation, they had to travel quite a distance before they could find a place to turn around in order to return to the restaurant to retrieve her glasses.

All the way back, the elderly husband became the classic grouchy old man. He fussed and complained and scolded his wife relentlessly during the entire return drive. The more he chided her, the more agitated he became. He just wouldn't let up one minute. To her relief, they finally arrived at the restaurant. As the woman got out of the car and hurried inside to retrieve her glasses, the old guy yelled to her, "While you're in there, you might as well get my hat."

"Every morning is the dawn of a new error."

THANKSGIVING DIVORCE

A man in Vancouver phoned his son in Regina a few days before the Thanksgiving weekend and said, "I hate to ruin your day son, but I have to tell you that your mother and I are divorcing. Thirty years of misery is enough."

"Pop, what are you talking about?" the son screams.

"We can't stand the sight of each other any longer," the father says. "We're sick of each other, and I'm sick of talking about this, so you call your sister in Chicago and tell her."

Frantic, the son calls his sister, who explodes on the phone. "They're getting divorced," she shouts, "I'll take care of this."

She calls Vancouver immediately, and screams at her father, "You are not getting divorced. Don't do a single thing until I get there. I'm calling my brother back, and we'll both be there tomorrow. Until then, don't do a thing. Do you hear me?" and she hangs up.

The man hangs up the phone and turns to his wife, "Okay dear," he says, "Let's go buy that turkey. They're both coming to visit us for Thanksgiving weekend and they're paying their own way."

"You can judge your age by the amount of pain you feel when you come in contact with a new idea." - John Nuveen

AGE IS JUST A FRAME OF MIND

Just a line to say I'm living, that I'm not among the dead
Though I'm getting more forgetful, and all mixed up in my head.

I got used to my arthritis, to my dentures I'm resigned
I can manage my bifocals, but dear God I miss my mind.

For sometimes I can't remember, when I stand at foot of stairs
If I must go up for something, or have I just come down from there?

And before the fridge so often, my poor mind is filled with doubt
Have I just put food away, or have I come to take it out?

And there's a time, when it is dark, I stop and hold my head
I don't know if I'm retiring, or am I getting out of bed?

So, if it's time to write you, there's no need for getting sore
I may think that I have written, and don't want to be a bore.

So remember that I love you, and wish that you were near
But now it's nearly mail time, so I must say "good-bye dear."

Here I stand before the mail box with a face so very red
Instead of mailing you my letter, I went and opened it instead.

DANGEROUS VOYAGE

The nearsighted elderly minister glanced at the note that Mrs. Brown had sent up with an usher. "George Brown having gone to sea, his wife desires the prayers of the congregation for his safety."

Failing to observe the punctuation, the minister startled his parishioners by announcing, "George Brown, having gone to see his wife, desires the prayers of the congregation for his safety."

"Hardening of the heart ages people more quickly than hardening of the arteries."

SECOND WIFE WAS YOUNGER

Evangelist Gypsy Smith was criticized for marrying a younger wife, after his first wife passed away. "Well," said Gypsy, "I'd rather wake up in the morning smelling perfume than liniment."

"Never regret growing old; many are denied that privilege."

"Always laugh when you can. It's cheap medicine." - Lord Byron

SHOP LIFTING

An 80 year old woman was arrested for shop lifting. When she went before the judge he asked her, "What did you steal?"

"I stole a can of peaches," she replied.

"Why did you steal a can of peaches?" asked the judge.

"Because I was hungry." she said.

"How many peaches were in the can?"

"Six," said the woman.

The judge then said, "Then I will give you six days in jail."

Before the judge could pronounce the sentence, the woman's husband spoke up, and asked the judge if he could say something.

The judge said, "What is it?"

The husband said, "She also stole a can of peas."

"Some people are so lazy that they won't know the difference when they retire."

SON-IN-LAW PERFORMS SURGERY

An older Jewish gentleman was on the operating table awaiting surgery. He had insisted that his son-in-law, a renowned surgeon, perform the operation. As he was about to get the anesthetic he asked to speak to his son-in-law.

"Yes, Dad, what is it?"

"Don't be nervous my boy, do your best and just remember, if it doesn't go well, if something happens to me, your mother-in-law is going to come and live with you and your wife."

"You may not have saved a lot of money in your life, but if you have saved a lot of heartaches for other folks, you are a pretty rich man." - Seth Parker

58

"You can close your eyes to reality but not to memories." - Stainslaw Lee

OIL OF DELAY

Mary had been visiting with her grandmother. When she came home she was all excited and said to her mother, "Mommy you said the other day that you wondered what grandma used to make her look so young. She told me what it is."

"What is it darling," asked Mary's mother.

"Grandma said she uses the Oil of Delay!"

"If I had known how wonderful grandchildren can be, I would have had them before I had my children." - Dr. J. Vernon McGee

KEEPING A SECRET

A man and woman had been married for more than 60 years. They had shared everything. They had talked about everything. They had kept no secrets from each other except that the little old woman had a shoe-box in the top of her closet that she had cautioned her husband never to open or ask her about.

For all of these years, he had never thought about the box, but one day the little old woman got very sick and the doctor said she would not recover. In trying to sort out their affairs, the little old man took down the shoe-box and took it to his wife's bedside. She agreed that it was time that he should know what was in the box.

When he opened it, he found two crocheted doilies and a stack of money totaling $15,000.00. He asked her about the contents. "When we were to be married," she said, "my grandmother told me the secret of a happy marriage was to never argue. She told me that if I ever got angry with you, I should just keep quiet and crochet a doily."

The little old man was so moved he had to fight back the tears. Only two precious doilies were in the box. She had only been angry with him two times in all those years of living and loving. He almost burst with happiness.

"Darling," he said, "that explains the doilies, but what about all of this money? Where did it come from?"

"Oh," she said, "That's the money I made from selling the doilies."

**"A truly happy person is one who can enjoy
the scenery on a detour."**

"We can't change the past, but we can ruin a perfectly good present by worrying about the future."

TAKE YOUR MEDICINE

A distraught senior citizen phoned her doctor's office. "Is it true," she wanted to know, "that the medication that you prescribed has to be taken for the rest of my life?"

"Yes, I'm afraid so," the doctor told her.

There was a moment of silence before the senior lady replied, "I'm wondering, then just how serious is my condition. This prescription is marked 'No refills'."

"You should always go to other's funerals otherwise they won't come to yours." - Yogi Berra

FROM ONE OCTOGENARIAN TO OTHER OCTOGENARIANS

"Don't allow yourself to feel old; don't give up your interest in life; cultivate a hobby, have a game now and then with your grandchildren, or someone else's; don't think about the end—God has lovingly planned that, and you will be as unaware of your passing out as you were of your coming in. I take it for granted, of course, that you have entrusted yourself to Christ for eternity."
- Dr. F. B. Meyer

"How old would you be if you didn't know how old you are?"

ESTATE PLANNING

Dan was a single guy living at home with his father and working in the family business. When he found out he was going to inherit a fortune when his sickly father died, he decided he needed a wife with which to share his fortune.

One evening at an investment meeting he spotted the most beautiful woman he had ever seen. Her natural beauty took his breath away. "I may look like just an ordinary man," he said to her, "but in just a few years, my father will die, and I'll inherit 20 million dollars."

Impressed, the woman obtained his business card and three weeks later, she became his stepmother.

Women are so much better at estate planning than men.

"Eventually you will reach a point when you stop lying about your age and start bragging about it."

FORGETFUL

An elderly couple was having a problem remembering things, so they decided to go to the doctor for a checkup. The doctor told them that they were physically okay, but they might want to start writing things down to help them remember.

Later that night, while watching TV, the old man got up from his chair. His wife asked, "Where are you going?"

"To the kitchen," he replied.

She asked, "Will you please get me a bowl of ice cream?"

The husband said, "Sure."

She gently reminded him. "Don't you think you should write it down so you can remember it?"

He said, "No, I can remember that!"

She then said, "Well, I'd liked some strawberries on top! You'd better write it down because I know you'll forget it. The doctor told us to write things down so we wouldn't forget."

He said, "I can remember that! You want a bowl of ice cream with strawberries."

She added, "I'd also like whipped cream. Now I'm certain you'll forget that, so you'd better write it down."

Irritated, he said, "I don't need to write it down. I can remember that! Ice cream with strawberries and whipped cream," he grumbled on his way into the kitchen.

After about 20 minutes the old man returned from the kitchen and handed his wife a plate of bacon and eggs. She stares at the plate for a moment and said, "You forgot my toast!"

"An old-timer is a fellow who remembers when it cost more to run a car than to park it."

GOOD EXCUSE FOR SPEEDING

Did you hear about the 83 year old woman who talked herself out of a speeding ticket by telling the young officer that she had exceeded the speed limit because she had to get there before she forgot where she was going?

"There's no reason to be the richest man in the cemetery." - Colonel Sanders

MEANINGFUL CONVERSATION

An old farmer walks into an attorney's office to file for a divorce.

Attorney: "May I help you?"

Farmer: "Yeah, I want to get one of those divorces."

Attorney: "Well, do you have any grounds?"

Farmer: "Yeah, I got about 140 acres."

Attorney: "No, you don't understand. Do you have a case?"

Farmer: "No, I don't have a Case, but I got a John Deere."

Attorney: "No, you still don't understand. I mean do you have a grudge?"

Farmer: "Yeah I got a grudge. That's where I park my John Deere."

Attorney: "No sir, I mean do you have a suit?"

Farmer: "Yes, sir. I got a suit. I wear it to church on Sundays."

Attorney: "Well, sir, does your wife beat you up or anything?"

Farmer: "Nope, we both get up about 4:30."

Attorney: "Okay, let me put it this way. Why do you want a divorce?"

Farmer: "Well, I can never have a meaningful conversation with her."

DOING TWO THINGS AT ONCE

The lady of the house had to go out on an errand at the time her favorite program of recipes was coming on television. She asked her retired husband to copy the recipes down for her. He was listening to a CD giving instructions for some exercises. This was the result:

Hands on hips, place 1 cup of flour on the shoulder. Raise knees and depress toes. Mix thoroughly in ½ cup milk. Repeat six times. Inhale quickly 1/2 tsp. baking powder, lower the feet and mash two hard boiled eggs in a bowl. Lay flat on the floor and roll in 2 egg whites backward and forward until it comes to a boil. In 10 minutes, remove from fire and rub smartly with a towel. Dress in warm flannels, and serve with tomato soup.

**"Birthdays are good for you.
The more you have, the longer you live."**

TWO OLD KINGS

King David and King Solomon led merry, merry lives,
With many, many lady friends and many, many wives.
And when old age crept over them with many, many qualms,
King Solomon wrote the Proverbs and King David wrote the Psalms

"Being old is a state of mind."

TOGETHER STILL

Let me hold your hand as we go downhill,
We've shared our strength and we share it still,
It hasn't been easy to make the climb,
But the way was eased by your hand in mine.

Like the lake, our life has had ripples too,
Ill health, and worries, and payments due,
With happy pauses along the way,
A graduation, a raise in pay.

At the foot of the slope we will stop and rest,
Look back, if you wish, we've been truly blessed.
We've been spared the grief of being torn apart
By death, or divorce, or a broken heart.

The view ahead is one of the best,
Just a little bit farther and then we can rest.
We move more slowly but together still,
Let me hold your hand as we go downhill.

WHAT IS YOUR LIFE?

Someone has described life as follows: "Youth is a struggle, maturity is a blunder, and old age is a regret." Life ought not to be that way. It should be enjoyable, fulfilling and a journey hand in hand with the eternal God. Unfortunately, many people approach their death bed and discover that they've never really lived. What is your life?

"If God is in charge and loves us, then whatever is given is subject to His control and is meant ultimately for our joy." - Elizabeth Elliot

63

AN AMISH TRANSFORMATION

An Amish boy and his father were in a department store for the very first time. They were amazed by almost everything they saw, but especially by two shiny, silver walls that could move apart and then slide back together again.

The boy asked, "What is that father?"

The father, never having seen an elevator, responded, "Son, I have never seen anything like that in my life. I don't know what it is."

While the boy and his father were watching in amazement, an overweight, very unattractive woman lumbered up to the moving walls and pressed a button. The walls opened and the woman walked between them and into a small room. Then the walls closed and the boy and his father watched the small circular numbers above the walls light up sequentially.

They continued to watch until it reached the last number and then the numbers began to light up in the reverse order. Finally the walls opened up again and a gorgeous slim young blonde stepped out. The father, not taking his eyes off the young woman, said quietly, "Son, go get your mother right now!"

JOINED THE FITNESS CLUB

I feel like my body has gotten totally out of shape, so I got my doctor's permission to join a fitness club and start exercising. I decided to take an aerobics class for seniors. I bent, twisted, gyrated, jumped up and down, and perspired for an hour. By the time I got my leotards on the class was over.

"I don't know how I got over the hill without getting to the top."

A 104 YEAR OLD

Reporters were interviewing a 104-year-old woman: "And what do you think is the best thing about being 104?" one reporter asked. She simply replied, "No peer pressure."

POET'S PRAYER

God's road is all uphill, but do not tire,
Rejoice that we may still, keep climbing higher.
- Arthur Guiterman

"Life is a compromise of what your ego wants to do, what experience tells you to do, and what your body allows you to do."

"All of life is preparation for the next chapter."

SHE'S NINETY YEARS OF AGE

With this brief communication
We offer our congratulation
For the birth registration
Says she's ninety years of age.

But with her demonstration
There is no justification
To give any confirmation
That she's ninety years of age.

Watch her daily presentations
Her amusingly gyrations
There are no indications
That she's ninety years of age.

When she makes a proclamation
Maybe with exaggeration,
We consider the occasion.
That she's ninety years of age.

Takes more time for preparation
Now and then some constipation
We forgive this situation
Cause she's ninety years of age.

We accept the calculation
Using our imagination
That she's in her generation
And she's ninety years of age.

So it seems with dedication
And unveiling revelation
We'll enjoy this celebration
She is ninety years of age.
                    - A. Daniel Goldsmith

"I'm not afraid to die, I'm kinda looking forward to it. I know the Lord has His arms wrapped around this big fat sparrow."
- Ethel Waters

GRANDMA'S ON A LONG WALK

My grandma started walking four miles each day when she was 55 years old. Now she is 78 and we have no idea where she is.

"One thing about getting older is that you can sing in the bathroom while brushing your teeth."

A GRANDSON'S DEFINITION OF THE HUMAN ANATOMY

The Bible reminds us that "out of the mouths of babes" great wisdom is sometimes brought forth. A young boy was asked in his school to define the human anatomy. He wrote the following essay.

"Your head is kinda round and hard, and brains are in it. Your hair is on it. Your face is in front of your head where you eat and make faces. Your neck is what keeps your head out of your collar. It's hard to keep clean. Your stummick is something that if you don't eat enough it hurts and spinach don't help none. Your spine is a long bone in your neck that keeps you from folding up. Your back is always behind you no matter how quick you turn around. Your arms you have to pitch with, and so you can reach the butter. Your fingers stick out of your hands so you can throw a curve and add up 'rithmetic. Your legs is what if you have not got two of, you can't get to first base. Your feet are what you run on; your toes are what always get stubbed. And that's all there is to you except what's inside, and I never saw it."

An interesting definition of a human being by a young boy. It no doubt causes us to smile, but there is vastly more to man than that which is seen on the outside. For every individual possesses a never-dying soul, that salvation for which the Lord Jesus Christ, God's only begotten Son, gave His life on Calvary's cross. The Bible tells us that the Lord is not willing that any should perish, but that all should come to repentance. You may be able to define all of the physical aspects of an individual, but the definition of God's remedy for the sickness of the soul can only be met through personal faith in the Savior, for the Bible rightly declares, "The soul that sinneth, it shall die."

FINISHED CHORES

Oma and Opa worked past the normal retirement age of 65. They were both busy professional people and had trouble finding time for chores and home maintenance. On weekends they each made a list of things to be done. Opa's list was never completely crossed off, but Oma's always was.

Puzzled, I asked her how she managed that. "Simple," she said with a satisfied grin. "I do the chore first, and then I write it on my list and cross it off."

"I'm really not getting older, I'm just more gifted chronologically." - A. Daniel Goldsmith

"It is by growing old that one learns to remain young."

NO MEN, THANK YOU

An elderly woman died last month. Having never married, she requested no male pallbearers. In her handwritten instructions for her memorial service, she wrote, "They wouldn't take me out while I was alive, so I don't want them to take me out when I'm dead."

**"The older we get, the fewer things seem
worth waiting in line for."**

OH HOW THEY LOVED EACH OTHER

A happy couple had always raised cucumbers and made sweet pickles together. The husband just loved to watch things grow. Thus he spent his winters studying the seed catalogues to get the best possible cucumbers. The whole family enjoyed preparing the soil, planting and caring for the plants. He would often go out and just enjoy the way they grew. His wife loved to make sweet pickles. She studied the best recipes and the best methods of preparing and preserving them. They were such a happy family, and all their visitors went home with a jar of their famous pickles. The church always had a good supply of their pickles as well. People marveled at this family that had found a project to do together.

Finally, the man died. The next spring all the children returned home. They said to their mother, "We know how much you love making pickles, so we are going to prepare the garden and plant them for you." The mother smiled and said, "Thanks a lot children, but you don't have to do any planting for I really don't enjoy pickle making. I only did that because your father loved to grow the cucumbers so much." The children were all amazed, but the youngest son was upset, because the father had pulled him aside not too long before and shared with him that he really didn't like growing cucumbers, but only did it to please the mother!

**"A sense of humor can help you overlook the unattractive,
tolerate the unpleasant, cope with the unexpected,
and smile through the unbearable."**

50th ANNIVERSARY COMING UP

A couple were about to celebrate their 50th wedding anniversary. The wife was hard of hearing. He was practicing his little speech that he was going to make. With a glass in his hand he lifted the same and said. "You've been tried and true." The wife who was sitting close by said, "And I'm tired of you, too."

"Being young is beautiful, but being old is comfortable."

CAN'T BELIEVE WE MADE IT

According to today's regulators and bureaucrats, those of us who were kids in the 30's, 40's, 50's, and even into the 60's probably shouldn't have survived.

Our baby cribs were covered with bright colored lead-based paint. We had no childproof lids or locks on medicine bottles, doors, or cabinets, and when we rode our bikes, we had no helmets, not to mention the risks we took when we hitchhiked.

As children, we would ride in cars with no seat belts or air bags. Riding in the back of a pickup truck on a warm day was always a special treat. We drank water from the garden hose and not from a bottle. Horrors! We ate cupcakes, bread and butter, and drank soda pop with sugar in it, but we were never overweight because we were always outside playing. We shared one soft drink with four friends, from one bottle, and no one actually died from this.

We would spend hours building our go-carts out of scraps and then rode down the hill, only to find out we forgot the brakes. After running into the bushes a few times, we learned to solve the problem.

We would leave home in the morning and play all day, as long as we were back when the street lights came on. No one was able to reach us all day. No cell phones. Unthinkable!

We did not have Play stations, Nintendo, X-Boxes, Wii Games, no 300 channels on cable, video or DVD movies, surround sound, personal computers, IPod, Blackberry, or internet chat rooms, and no text messaging. We had friends! We went outside and found them.

We played dodge ball, and sometimes, the ball would really hurt. We fell out of trees, got cut and broke bones and teeth, and there were no lawsuits from these accidents. No one was to blame but us. We had fights and punched each other and got black and blue and learned to get over it. We made up games with sticks and tennis balls, and although we were told it would happen, we did not put out any eyes. We rode bikes or walked to a friend's home and knocked on the door, or rang the bell or just walked in and talked to them.

Little League had tryouts and not everyone made the team. Those who didn't had to learn to deal with disappointment. Some students weren't as smart as others, so they failed a grade and were held back to repeat the same grade. Tests were not adjusted for any reason. Our actions were our own. Consequences were expected. The idea of parents bailing us out if we got into trouble in school or broke a law was unheard of. They actually sided with the school or the law.

This generation has produced some of the best risk-takers, problem solvers, and inventors, ever. We had freedom, failure, success, and responsibility, and we learned how to deal with it.

"Fear not that thy life shall come to an end, but rather fear that it shall never have a beginning." - Cardinal Newman

"If things get better with age, then I'm approaching magnificent."

I WALKED A MILE

I walked a mile with pleasure, she chatted all the way,
But left me none the wiser, for all she had to say.
I walked a mile with sorrow and not a word said she,
But oh the things I learned from her, when sorrow walked with me.

HOLDING HANDS

While at the mall, I saw an elderly couple holding hands while they were walking. As they approached, I commented on how romantic it was.

He replied, "We have been holding hands when we go out in public for over thirty years. I have to. If I let go, she shops."

ARE YOU LIVING?

There was a very cautious man
Who never laughed or played;
He never risked, he never tried,
He never sang or prayed.
And when he one day passed away
His insurance was denied;
For since he never really lived,
They claimed he never died!

"Worry is like a rocking chair: it gives you something to do but will get you nowhere."

✗GOD MADE ME

A little girl was sitting on her grandfather's lap as he read her a bedtime story. From time to time, she would take her eyes off the book and reach up to touch his wrinkled cheek. She was alternately stroking her own cheek, then his again. Finally she spoke up, "Grandpa, did God make you?"

"Yes, sweetheart," he answered, "God made me a long time ago."

"Oh," she paused, "Grandpa, did God make me too?"

"Yes, indeed, honey," he said, "God made you just a little while ago."

Feeling their respective faces again, she observed, "God's getting better at it, isn't He?"

**"When you are dissatisfied with your age and would like
to go back to your youth, think about algebra."**

TWO FINAL REQUESTS

An elderly woman decided to prepare her will and told her preacher she had two final requests. First, she wanted to be cremated, and second, she wanted her ashes scattered over Wal-Mart. "Wal-Mart?" the preacher exclaimed. "Why Wal-Mart?"

"Then I'll be sure my daughters visit me twice a week," she replied.

**"So long as one continues to be amazed,
one can delay growing old."**

WE DID IT WITH COUPONS

A quaint elderly couple were showing some friends through their 12-room house. They proudly announced that they had built the house with premiums redeemed for soap coupons. They showed them through the living room, the dining room, the kitchen, the bathroom, and one bedroom. They explained how many soap coupons they had to use for each chair, table, bed, carpet, etc.

At the end of the tour, their friends said, "You've only shown us five of the twelve rooms, what about the other seven?"

"Oh, those," shrugged the couple. "That's where we keep the soap."

EAGER TO LEARN

Howard Hendricks, a professor at Dallas Theological Seminary told about a lady who attended a Sunday School Convention in Chicago. He said, "I saw a lady with a convention badge at the little hamburger stand where three of us fellows were having lunch. We invited her to join us for our snack."

"I guessed her age to be 65," says Hendricks, "but she was actually 83. She said that she taught Junior High boys. We found out later that she had a class of 50 boys. She lived in Upper Michigan on a pension, and had saved pennies to get a bus ticket to Chicago on an all-night trip just to attend the Convention."

She told Professor Hendricks and his friends, "I came to see if I could learn something that would make me a better teacher."

"We felt like crawling out under the door of the hamburger house," said Hendricks.

"The person who considers himself too old to learn something has probably always been that way."

PULPIT SUPPLY

As a retired pastor, I often filled in for a pastor who was absent from his pulpit, which is often referred to as "pulpit supply." One Sunday morning after preaching in a small country church, the treasurer thanked me profusely and gave me a check for one hundred dollars.

"I appreciate the opportunity to fill in as needed," I said to the treasurer, "but I would like to donate this money to your church and maybe you could use it in a special project."

"That would be wonderful!" said the treasurer. "We have just started a special fund recently and I would be happy to put your money towards the same. We're trying to raise some money so that we can afford better speakers."

PHOTOS OF THE GRANDSON

A man said to a friend, "Have I ever told you about my grandson and shown you pictures of him?"

The friend replied, "No, you haven't, and I want to thank you for it!"

"I'm not a senior citizen. I am a citizen with seniority."
- A. Daniel Goldsmith

SETTLED THE ARGUMENT

The other day, Grandma and Grandpa got into a little argument. Grandpa said it was petty. Grandma would have said it was an Armageddon. As is human nature, neither of them would admit the possibility that they might be in error.

To her credit, Grandma finally said, "Look. I'll tell you what. I'll admit I'm wrong if you admit that I was right.

"Fine," said Grandpa.

Grandma took a deep breath, looked him straight in the eye and said, "I'm wrong."

He grinned and replied, "You're right."

"If someone declares that he is able to do everything at sixty that he was able to do at twenty, then he was not doing very much when he was twenty."

71

OLD GOATS

A group of Americans were traveling by tour bus through Holland.   As they stopped at a cheese farm a young guide led them through the process of cheese making, explaining that they used goat's milk. She showed the group a lovely hillside where many goats were grazing.

"These," she explained "are the older goats put out to pasture when they no longer produce." She then asked, "What do you do in America with your old goats?"

A spry old gentleman answered, "They send us on bus tours!"

BUILDING A BARBECUE

A recent retiree and his wife sold their home and moved into their first condominium. He went into the local building supply store and ordered 4,800 bricks.

"May I ask what you're building?" asks the clerk behind the counter.

"It's going to be a barbecue."

"Wow, that's a lot of bricks for one barbecue,"

"Not really," said the retiree, "we live on the 12th floor."

"Old age is when your memory is shorter and your stories are longer."

TRAGEDIES INTO TRIUMPHS

There are times when we have our trials and it is only after having gone through the same that we see God was at work, even though we were not too joyful. Vance Havner in his book "*It Is Toward Evening*" tells the story about the small town of Enterprise, Alabama that made its living entirely from growing cotton. It was not a great living, but it was a living. Calamity struck when the boll weevil invaded the community and threatened to ruin everyone. As it turns out, the farmers were forced to switch to peanuts and other crops that eventually brought them greater return than they would have made with cotton. Ultimately that which had seemed a disaster became the basis for undreamed prosperity. To register their appreciation, they erected a monument to the boll-weevil. To this very day in that little Southern town that monument stands. We all have boll-weevil experiences: financial reversals, professional failures, relational disappointments, psychological or physical hurts. These trials can bump us out of our old ways and force us to find new ways to live. Many tragedies can turn to triumphs through the Lord.

"Using your few days wisely can make an eternal difference."

"Nothing is more often opened by mistake than the mouth."

ONE HUNDRED

A friend asked a lady how old she was. She replied, "One hundred."

"Well," said the friend, "I doubt that you'll see another hundred."

The lady responded by saying, "I don't know about that. I am stronger today at one hundred than I was when I started the first hundred."

THE WOODEN LEG

A Free Methodist was working in a gold mine and was involved in an accident. They took him to a Catholic Hospital and a Pentecostal surgeon amputated his leg.

A Presbyterian woman felt sorry for him so she put an ad in the Mennonite Herald advertising for a wooden leg. A Christian & Missionary Alliance woman read the Presbyterian woman's ad in the Mennonite Herald about the Free Methodist in the Catholic Hospital whose leg had been amputated by a Pentecostal surgeon.

Her husband had been a Baptist but he was dead now, and he had had a wooden leg which he had left behind. So she called the Salvation Army and they sent a Captain to the Christian & Missionary Alliance woman's house and picked up the Baptist leg and took it to the Express office and gave it to the Lutheran express office operator who took it up to the Catholic Hospital and handed it to the Christian Reformed nurse who strapped the Baptist leg on the Free Methodist and made A UNITED BRETHREN OUT OF HIM.

"Live so the preacher won't have to lie at your funeral."

HUSBAND FORGOT ANNIVERSARY

A husband was in BIG trouble when he forgot his wedding anniversary. "Tomorrow," his wife angrily told him, "there had better be something in our driveway that goes from zero to 200 in two seconds flat!"

The next morning, the wife looked outside and saw a small package in the driveway. She brought it inside, opened it, and found a brand new bathroom scale.

The man is hoping to be discharged from the hospital by the end of the week, but will not have his full sight restored for another week or ten days.

"A smile is a curve that sets many things straight."

ENGAGED TO BE MARRIED

Jacob, age 92, and Rebecca, age 89, are all excited about their decision to get married. They went for a stroll to discuss the wedding and on the way they passed a pharmacy. Jacob suggests that they go in. Jacob addresses the man behind the counter: "Are you the owner?"

The pharmacist answers "Yes".

"We're about to get married," says Jacob. "Do you sell heart medication?"

"Of course we do," says the pharmacist.

"How about medicine for circulation?"

"All kinds."

"Do you have medicine for rheumatism, scoliosis? "

"Definitely," replies the pharmacist.

"How about medicine for memory problems, arthritis, and jaundice?"

The answer was, "Yes, a large variety. The works."

Jacob asked, "What about vitamins, sleeping pills, Geritol, antidotes for Parkinson's disease?"

"Absolutely," was the reply.

"One more question," Jacob asked, "Do you sell wheelchairs and walkers?"

"All speeds and sizes."

Jacob says to the pharmacist, "We'd like to register here for our wedding gifts, please."

SENIOR EXERCISES

I started by standing outside behind the house and with a 5-pound potato sack in each hand, I extended my arms straight out to my sides and held them there as long as I could. After a while, I moved up to a 10-pound potato sack, then a 50-pound potato sack, and finally, I got to where I could lift a 100-pound potato sack in each hand and hold my arms straight out for more than a full minute!

Tomorrow, I am going to start putting a few potatoes in the sacks.

YOU'VE ATTENDED CHURCH FOR MANY YEARS
IF YOU REMEMBER

- When families sat together in church.
- When guitar playing was mainly country and western music.
- When hymnals were common and parishioners sang four part harmony.
- When churches had choirs and choirs wore robes.
- When chewing gum in church was disrespectful.
- When talking in church meant whispering a prayer before the service.
- When the pastor walked to the back of the church to greet the parishioners.
- When a week of evangelistic meetings was common and we never missed one night.
- When the whole family came to hear a missionary.
- When ladies wore dresses and hats and men wore suits and ties.
- When visiting in a home after church meant gathering around the piano and singing.
- When pastors preached often about "Heaven" and "Hell."
- When a sermon on "The Second Coming" attracted a large crowd.
- When an invitation to the altar was given at every service.
- When pastors visited parishioners and could call them by name.
- When a child gave up their bed so the visiting preacher could stay in a home.
- When the Sunday School picnic was a highlight of the year.
- When "Sword Drills" were common and "Scripture Memorization" was encouraged.
- When reading the Bible through in a year was a New Year's goal.
- When we all used the same Bible translation.

- A. Daniel Goldsmith

HE KNEW THE ANSWER

While attending a seniors marriage seminar on communications, the husband, who had enjoyed 55 years of marriage listened to the instructor declare, "It is essential that husbands and wives know the things that are important to each other."

He addressed the husbands, "Can you describe your wife's favorite flower?"

He leaned over, touched his wife's arm gently and whispered, "Pillsbury All-Purpose, isn't it?"

"You can't do much about your ancestors, but you can influence your descendants enormously."

A SENSE OF HUMOR

When a retired missionary was asked what he would pack in his suitcase if he were to return to his overseas missionary ministry, he quickly responded by saying "A sense of humor." Another missionary said, "You need two things if you want to be happy in God's work overseas, "A good sense of humor and no sense of smell."

A KEEPER

I grew up in the 40's with a practical parent, my mother, God love her, who ironed Christmas wrapping paper and reused it, and who washed aluminum foil after she cooked in it, then reused it. She was the original recycle queen, before they had a name for it.

It was the time for fixing things...a curtain rod, the kitchen radio, the screen door, the oven door, the hem in a dress. Things we keep. It was a way of life, and sometimes it made me crazy. All that re-fixing, reheating, renewing, I wanted just once to be wasteful. Waste meant affluence. Throwing things away meant you knew there'd always be more.

But then my mother died, and I sat in my kitchen that Sunday afternoon reading her old handmade cookbook in a binder. I was struck with the pain of feeling all alone, learning that sometimes there isn't any more. Sometimes, what we care about most gets all used up and goes away, never to return.

So while we have it, it's best we love it, and care for it, and fix it when it's broken, and heal it when it's sick. This is true for marriage, and old cars, and children with bad report cards, and dogs with bad hips, and aging parents and grandparents. We keep them because they are worth it; because we are worth it.

Some things we keep. Like a best friend that moved away or a classmate we grew up with. There are just some things that make life important, like people we know who are special, and so, we keep them close!

"Yesterday is history. Tomorrow is a mystery. And today? Today is a gift, that's why we call it the present."

SPEEDING TICKET

An elderly person was stopped after doing 73 mph. When told he was getting a ticket, he asked the officer, "Is there a senior citizen's discount?"

MY GREATEST COMPLIMENT

The greatest compliment that I ever received for a sermon which I preached was given to me when I was just a student in Bible College. I was asked to preach one Sunday morning at a little Baptist Church that was being served by a student pastor from a nearby university.

This older lady spoke to me after the service and said, "I guess you must not be very educated. I understood everything that you said."   - A. Daniel Goldsmith

"Old age comes at a bad time."

"A lot of life insurance policies cost a great deal of money to maintain. But look on the bright side, when you die, you'll be rich !"

BEING BOSSED AROUND

A mild-mannered man, who recently retired, was tired of being bossed around by his wife; so he went to a psychiatrist. The psychiatrist said he needed to build his self-esteem, and so gave him a book on assertiveness, which he read within hours.

When he had finished reading the book, the man stormed into the house and walked up to his wife. Pointing a finger in her face, he said, "From now on, I want you to know that I am the man of this house, and my word is law! I want you to prepare me a gourmet meal tonight, and when I'm finished eating my meal, I expect a sumptuous dessert afterward. Then, after dinner, you're going to fill the bath tub with warm water so I can relax. And when I'm finished with my bath, guess who's going to dress me and comb my hair?"

"The funeral director," said his wife.

"Don't cry because you are getting older and the end of life is getting closer, smile because it happened."

STATE OF THE ART

Two men were chatting at the senior citizens center. One told his friend that he had just bought a new hearing aid. "It cost me four thousand dollars, but it is state of the art. It's perfect."

"Really," replied his friend. "What kind is it?"

"It's twelve thirty!"

OLD AGE IS BEAUTIFUL

- ■ It is the old apple trees that are decked with the loveliest blossoms.
- ■ It is the ancient redwoods that rise to majestic heights.
- ■ It is the old violins that produce the richest tones.
- ■ It is the ancient coins, stamps and furniture that people seek.
- ■ It is the old friends who are loved the best.
- ■ Thank God for the blessings of age and the wisdom, patience and maturity that goes with it. Old age is beautiful.

"People go through two basic stages of life: Young trying to be older and the older trying to be young." - Daniel Neal

**"When you are young, you do a lot of wishful thinking,
but when you are old you do a lot of thoughtful wishing."**

BUT NOT TODAY

I shall grow old perhaps, but not today, not while my hopes are young, my spirit strong,
My vision clear, because life has a way of smoothing out the wrinkles with a song.

I shall grow old, perhaps, but not today, not while my dreams remain a shining shield,
My faith a lance, and 'neath a sky of grey, my colors wave upon the battlefield.

I shall grow old, perhaps, but not today, not while this pen can write upon a page,
And memories turn winter into May, shall this stout heart be brought to terms by age?

I shall grow old, perhaps, but not today, and scorning time who would enlist my tears,
I stand convinced there is a better way, of occupying all the coming years.

I shall grow old, perhaps, but not today, in my own style and in my own sweet time,
No night so dark there does not fall a ray of light along the pathway that I climb.

Just say of me, when my last hour slips like one bright leaf to softly rest among
The others..."Life was summer to the heart, of one who died believing she was young."
- Grace E. Easley

"No retiree has ever been shot while helping his wife with the dishes."

STRENGTH & BEAUTY

"God planned the strength and beauty of youth to be physical, but the strength and beauty of age is spiritual. We gradually lose the strength and beauty that is temporary so we'll be sure to concentrate on the strength and beauty that is forever." - Dr. Robertson McQuilkin

"Some people mellow with age, others simply go rotten."

POTTED GERANIUMS

"Sorry, we don't have potted geraniums," the clerk said, and then added helpfully, "Could you use African violets?"

"No," replied the poor old fellow, "It was geraniums my wife told me to water while she was gone."

"Don't take life too seriously you'll never get out of it alive.

"To make a long story short, don't tell it."

A WILD NIGHT AT OUR HOUSE

Another year has passed and we all are a little older
Last summer felt hotter and winter seems much colder.
I rack my brain for happy thoughts, to put down on my pad,
But lots of things that come to mind just make me kind of sad.
There was a time not long ago when life was quite a blast.
Now I fully understand about "Living in the Past".
We used to go to friends homes, football games and lunches.
Now we go to therapy, hospitals, and after-funeral brunches.
We used to go out dining, and couldn't get our fill.
Now we ask for doggie bags, come home and take a pill.
We used to often travel to places near and far.
Now we get backaches from riding in the car.
We used to go out shopping for new clothing at the Mall
But now we never bother, all the sizes are too small.
That, my friend is how life is and now my tale is told.
So, enjoy each day and live it up, before you get too old!!

"Middle age is when a person has stopped growing at both ends and is now growing in the middle."

AGING IS WHEN

1. Everything hurts and what doesn't hurt, doesn't work.
2. The gleam in your eye is the sun hitting your bifocals.
3. You feel like the night after, but you haven't been anywhere.
4. Your little black book contains only names ending in M.D.
5. You get winded playing chess.
6. Your children begin to look middle-aged.
7. You join a health club, but don't go.
8. "25 Years Ago Today", is your favorite part of the newspaper.
9. You sit in a rocking chair and can't get it going.
10. Your knees buckle and your belt won't.
11. The best part of the day is over when the alarm clock goes off.
12. Your back goes out more often than you do.
13. You sink your teeth into a steak and they stay there.
14. People ask if your wife is your daughter.
15. Birthdays no longer matter.

"There's a smile down inside of you that is just dying to come out. It won't until you give yourself permission." - Bill Cosby

FORTY YEARS OF MARRIAGE

A married couple in their early 60s were celebrating their 40th wedding anniversary in a quiet romantic little restaurant. Suddenly, a tiny yet beautiful fairy appeared on their table. She said, "For being such an exemplary married couple and for loving each other for all these years, I will grant you each a wish."

The wife answered, "Oh, I want to travel around the world with my darling husband." The fairy waved her magic wand and – poof! Two tickets for the Queen Mary II appeared in her hands.

The husband thought for a moment: "Well, this is all very romantic, but an opportunity like this will never come again. I'm sorry my love, but my wish is to have a wife 30 years younger than me." The wife and the fairy were deeply disappointed, but a wish is a wish. So the fairy waved her magic wand and poof! The husband became 92 years old.

"You may be only one person in the world, but you may also be the world to one person."

AFRAID OF THE FUTURE

Corrie Ten Boom used to tell how when she was once afraid of the future, her father reminded her that when she went on a train trip as a small girl, he gave her the train ticket the day she started out, when she needed it, and not a long time before. God will give us what we need, when we need it.

THEY WILL PAY FOR THEMSELVES

Last year I replaced several windows in my house. They were the expensive double-insulated energy efficient windows. This week I got a call from the contractor complaining that the work has been done for a year and I had failed to pay for them. Boy, oh boy, did we go 'round and 'round. I told him no one pulls a fast one on this little old lady. Even though I am a senior citizen and used to be a blonde, doesn't mean that I am automatically stupid! I proceeded to tell him just what his salesman told me last year, that, "in one year they would pay for themselves".

EXPLAINING THE PRESCRIPTION

After giving an older woman a full medical examination, the doctor explained his prescription as he wrote it out. "When you get up, take the green pill with two glasses of water. Take the blue pill with two glasses of water after lunch. Take the red pill with two glasses of water after supper. Then just before going to bed take the brown pill with two glasses of water."

"Exactly what is my problem, doctor?" she asked.

"You're not drinking enough water," he said.

GOAT FOR DINNER

The young couple invited their elderly pastor for Sunday dinner. While they were in the kitchen preparing the meal, the minister asked their son what they were having. "Goat," the little boy replied.

"Goat?" replied the startled man of the cloth, "Are you sure about that?"

"Yep," said the youngster. "I heard Dad say to Mom, 'Today is just as good as any to have the old goat for dinner'."

"Old golfers never die; they just tee off and putt away."

FOUR SCORE AND TEN

One score and ten was not the end
But close to the beginning;
You knew a lot, or so you thought,
Married with kids and winning.

Two score and ten you began to send
Your children off to marry;
They needed money, you sought to lend
It nearly drove you hairy.

Three score and ten, your knees didn't bend
To doctor you did go;
Sitting long did hurt rear end
And your middle began to show.

Four score and ten is where you're at
You've seen it, done it all;
The hardest thing you now work at
Is trying to recall.

So if you can't remember when
Focus on what's ahead;
Remember you're four score and ten
You're living, you're not dead!
- A. Daniel Goldsmith

"Experience is the thing you have left when everything else is gone"

"Yesterday is just a cancelled check. Tomorrow is a promissory note. Today has all the cash you can handle. Spend it wisely."
- Dr. Adrian Rogers

A SENIOR'S MUSICAL ABILITIES

My parents recently retired! Mom always wanted to learn to play the piano, so Dad bought her a piano for her birthday. A few weeks later, I asked how she was doing with it. "Oh, we returned the piano" said my Dad, "I persuaded her to switch to a clarinet instead."

"How come?" I asked.

"Because with the Clarinet, she can't sing!"

"The trouble with the younger generation is that too many of us don't belong to it anymore."

I'VE ONLY BEGUN TO LIVE

Down in Texas some time ago, I happened to pick up a newspaper. It called me "Old Moody." Honestly, I never got such a shock from any paper in my life.

I went to my hotel and looked in the looking glass. I cannot conceive of getting old. I have a life that is never going to end! Death may change my position but not my condition, not my standing with Jesus Christ. Death is not going to separate us.

Old! I wish you all felt as young as I do here tonight. Why I am only 62 years old! If you meet me ten million years hence, then I will still be young. Read the 91st Psalm, verse 16: "With long life will I satisfy him."

That doesn't mean 70 years. Would that satisfy you? Did you ever see a man or woman of 70 satisfied? Don't they want to live longer? You know that 70 wouldn't satisfy you. Would 80? Would 90? Would 100? If Adam lived to be a million years old and then had to die, he wouldn't have been satisfied.

"With long life will I satisfy him"- life without end! Don't call me old. I am only 62. I have only begun to live!   - Evangelist Dwight L. Moody

"The only person who is not afraid to die is the person who is not afraid to live." - General Douglas MacArthur

"Don't let what you can't control keep you from enjoying what you can enjoy." - Dr. David Jeremiah

TEN SIGNS OF AGING

1. Your supply of brain cells is finally down to a manageable size.
2. Your secrets are safe with your friends because they can't remember them either.
3. Your joints are more accurate meteorologists than the national weather service.
4. People call at 9:00pm and ask, "Did I wake you?"
5. There is nothing left to learn the hard way.
6. Things you buy now won't wear out.
7. You can eat dinner at 4:00pm.
8. You have a party and the neighbors don't even realize it.
9. You no longer think of speed limits as a challenge.
10. Your eyes won't get much worse.

"Be nice to your kids, they'll be choosing your nursing home."

SENIOR'S EXERCISE PROGRAM

Beating around the bush; Jumping to conclusions; Climbing the walls; Swallowing my pride; Passing the buck; Throwing my weight around; Dragging my heels; Pushing my luck; Making Mountains out of molehills; Hitting the nail on the head; Wading through paperwork; Bending over backwards; Jumping on the bandwagon; Balancing the books; Eating crow; Running around in circles; Tooting my own horn; Pulling out the stops; Adding fuel to the fire; Climbing the ladder of success; Opening a can of worms; Putting my foot in my mouth.

Whew! What a workout! I think I'll exercise caution now, and sit down.

FASCINATED BY THE ELDERLY

While working for an organization that delivers lunches to elderly shut-ins, I used to take my 4-year old daughter on my afternoon rounds. She was unfailingly intrigued by the various appliances of old age, particularly the canes, walkers and wheelchairs. One day I found her staring at a pair of false teeth soaking in a glass. As I braced myself for the inevitable barrage of questions, she merely turned and whispered, "The tooth fairy will never believe this!"

"Humor is to life what shock absorbers are to automobiles."
- Sam Toler

THE NEW NEIGHBOR

Gramps new neighbor phoned him and awakened him one morning at 4:00am. "Your dog's barking and is keeping me awake," said the irritated neighbor. Gramps thanked him politely and asked for his name before hanging up.

The next morning at 4:00am Gramps called this neighbor and said, "Sir, I don't have a dog."

**"Good old days exist only in the minds of people
who avoid living in the present."**

WHEN I WAS YOUNGER

When I was in my younger days, I weighed a few pounds less,
I needn't hold my tummy in to wear a belted dress.
But now that I am older, I've set my body free;
There's comfort of elastic where once my waist would be.
Inventor of those high-heeled shoes, my feet have not forgiven;
I have to wear a nine now, but used to wear a seven.

And how about those pantyhose, they're sized by weight, you see,
So how come when I put them on the crotch is at my knees?
I need to wear these glasses as the prints are getting smaller;
And it wasn't very long ago I know that I was taller.
Though my hair has turned to silver and my skin no longer fits,
On the inside, I'm the same old me, just the outside's changed a bit.
- Maya Angelou

**"Many school class reunions today resemble
a geriatric convention."** - A. Daniel Goldsmith

FOUR LITTLE WORDS

Grandma and her sister Mary, both widows hadn't seen each other in awhile, so they decided to meet for lunch. The talk naturally got around to their respective love lives. Grandma's sister Mary confided that there really wasn't anyone special in her life, and figured that she would continue to be a widow.

Grandma, on the other hand, was beaming about the new widower that she had found. "He's perfect. He's handsome, he's sweet, and he still drives a car. Last night when we went out to dinner and he said the four little words I've been waiting to hear him say to me!"

"Did he say 'will you marry me'?" Mary asked.

Grandma replied, "No, he said 'put your money away'."

WHERE WILL YOU RETIRE

An old native of Arkansas said: "You can say what you want about the South, but I ain't never heard of any Southerner wanting to retire in the North."

BURIAL ARRANGEMENTS

It was a difficult subject to bring before his aged mother, but John felt that he must: "Mom, you're no longer a spring chicken and you do need to think ahead of what'll happen in the future. Why don't we make arrangements about when...you know...when...you pass on?" The mother didn't say anything, just sat there staring ahead.

"I mean, Mom, like...how do you want to finally go? Do you want to be buried or cremated?"

There was yet another long pause. Then the mother looked up and said, "Son, why don't you surprise me?"

"My memory's not as sharp as it used to be.
Also, my memory's not as sharp as it used to be."

REFLECTIONS OF AN OCTOGENARIAN

I'm reading more and dusting less. I'm sitting in the yard and admiring the view without fussing about the weeds in the garden. I'm spending more time with my family and friends and less time working. Whenever possible, life should be a pattern of experiences to savor, not to endure. I'm trying to recognize these moments now and cherish them.

I'm not "saving" anything; we use our good china and crystal for every special event such as losing a pound, getting the sink unstopped, or the first amaryllis blossom. I wear my good blazer to the market. My theory is if I can shell out $28.49 for one small bag of groceries, I might as well look prosperous. I'm not saving my good perfume for special parties, but wear it for clerks in the hardware store and tellers at the bank.

"Someday" and "one of these days" are losing their grip on my vocabulary. If it's worth seeing or hearing or doing, I want to see and hear and do it NOW. I'm not sure what others would've done had they known they wouldn't be here for the tomorrow that we all take for granted. But I think they would have called family members and a few close friends. They might also have called a few former friends to apologize and mend fences for past squabbles. I like to think they would have gone out for a Chinese dinner or for what ever their favorite restaurant was. I'm guessing. I'll never know.

It's those little things left undone that would make me angry if I knew my hours were limited, angry because I hadn't written certain letters which I had intended to write "one of these days". Angry and sorry that I didn't tell my husband and parents often enough, how much I truly love them. I'm trying very hard not to put off, hold back, or save anything that would add laughter and luster to our lives. And every morning when I open my eyes, I tell myself that it is special. Every day, every minute, every breath should be treasured.

"If you live wrong, you can't die right." - Evangelist Billy Sunday

WHO AM I

Art Linkletter tells the story about the time he visited a home for the elderly. He was a little taken aback because the people there did not seem to recognize him or know anything about him. But when he saw one bright eyed old lady smiling at him, he thought things were finally going his way. He said to her "Do you know who I am?" to which she replied, "No, but if you ask at the desk over there, they will tell you your name."

BLESSED BE NUTHIN'

Blessed be nuthin' remarked the wise sage.
Be glad if you've nuthin' in this day and age;
For nuthin' is sumpthin' that cannot be stole
Nor drop from your pocket or purses small hole.
Nuthin' is sumpthin' the bank cannot lose
The creditors seize nor the burglars abuse.
Folks who have nuthin' really should love it,
For nuthin' is sumpthin' the neighbors won't covet.
Nuthin' is sumpthin' that won't collect dust:
You don't have to hide it or protect it from rust.
So if you have nuthin' be glad – sing a song!
For when leaving this earth, you can take it along!

"If you can find a path with no obstacles, it probably doesn't lead anywhere." - Frank A. Clark

CLIMB THE WALL

"Oh, I sure am happy to see you," the little boy said to his grandmother on his mother's side. "Now maybe Daddy will do the trick he has been promising us."

The grandmother was curious. "What trick is that?" she asked.

"I heard him tell Mommy," the little boy answered, "that he would climb the wall if you came to visit".

PROBLEMS OF AGING

Several years ago the US Congress did a study on the problems of aging. They spent almost two million dollars on this study. Their significant conclusion, after a year and a half of study, was this, "The longer you live the older you get." Sounds like government expenditures.

"You don't have to be listed in Who's Who to know What's What."

"Nothing is more disgraceful than that an old man should leave nothing to prove that he has lived a long time, except his years."

COMPLIMENTING GRANDMA

I have never had a reputation for being a fantastic cook. I fed nourishing meals to my children and grandchildren, but not gourmet style. One evening I worked particularly hard on a new recipe, and once again it didn't turn out as well as I'd hoped.

My grandson, who is always sweet and very conscious of my feelings, chose his words carefully after the meal. "Grandma," he said, "that dinner was so good I thought someone else made it."

FINDERS KEEPERS

An elderly couple, who were childhood sweethearts and had settled down in their old neighborhood, were celebrating their fiftieth wedding anniversary. They walked down the street to their old school. They held hands as they found the old desk that they'd shared and where he had carved, "I love you, Sally."

On their way back home, an armored car drove by and a bag of money fell out of the armored car practically at their feet. Sally quickly picked it up, but they didn't know what to do with it so they took it home. At home, she counted the money, and it was fifty thousand dollars. The husband said, "We've got to give it back." She said, "Finders keepers." She put the money back in the bag and hid it up in their attic.

The next day, two FBI men went door-to-door in the neighborhood looking for the money and they showed up at their home. One of the agents said, "Pardon me, but did either of you find any money that fell out of an armored car yesterday?"

She said "No."

The husband said, "She's lying. She hid it up in the attic."

She said, "Don't believe him, he's getting senile."

So the agents sat the man down and began to question him. One of the FBI agents said, "Tell us the story from the beginning."

The old man said, "Well, when Sally and I were walking home from school yesterday..."

The FBI guy looked at his partner and said, "Let's get out of here."

"You know you're getting older when it takes more time to recover than it did to tire out." - Milton Berle

87

"Retirement should be based on the tread, not the mileage." - A. Ludden

DREADING OLD AGE

I have always dreaded old age. I cannot imagine anything worse than being old. How awful it must be to have nothing to do all day long but stare at the walls or watch TV. So last week, when the mayor suggested we all celebrate Senior Citizen Week by cheering up a senior citizen, I determined to do just that.

I would call on my new neighbor, an elderly retired gentleman, recently widowed, who, I presumed, had moved in with his married daughter because he was too old to take care of himself. I baked a batch of brownies, and, without bothering to call (some old people cannot hear the phone), I went off to brighten this old guy's day.

When I rang the doorbell this "old guy" came to the door dressed in tennis shorts and a polo shirt, looking about as ancient and decrepit as Donny Osmond. "I'm sorry I can't invite you in," he said when I introduced myself, "but I'm due at the Racquet Club at two. I'm playing in the semi-finals today.

"Oh, that's all right," I said. "I baked you some brownies…"

"Great!" he interrupted, snatching the box. "Just what I need for bridge club tomorrow! Thanks so much!"

"I just thought we'd visit a while. But that's okay! I'll just trot across the street and call on Granny Grady…"

"Don't bother," he said. "Granny's not home; I know. I just called to remind her of our date to go dancing tonight. She may be at the beauty shop. She mentioned at breakfast that she had an appointment for a tint job."

I called my Mother's cousin (age 83); she was in the hospital – working in the gift shop. I called my aunt (age 74); she was on vacation in China. I called my husband's uncle (age 79). I forgot; he was on his honeymoon.

still dread old age, now more than ever. I just don't think I'm up to it.

"Old age is fifteen years older than I am."

MY WIFE'S WORDS OF WISDOM

I was bemoaning the fact that I was tired and it was only noon. My wife, with her unique use of the English language said to me: "Many people our age are dead. Be thankful you were able to get up this morning so that you can have a nap." - A. Daniel Goldsmith

NOT GALLANT

Her husband didn't help her on the bus. "You're not as gallant as you were when I was a gal," she said playfully.

"And I'm not as buoyant as I was when I was a boy," he retorted.

"Aging has its pains and pleasures."
- A. Daniel Goldsmith

WASHING CLOTHES RECIPE

Years ago an Alabama grandmother gave her granddaughter, a new bride, the following recipe for washing clothes. This recipe is just the way grandma spelled it out.

Build fire in backyard to heat kettle of rain water. Set tubs so smoke wont blow in eyes if wind is pert. Shave one hole cake of lie soap in boilin water.

Sort things, make 3 piles; 1 pile white, 1 pile colored, 1 pile work britches and rags.

To make starch, stir flour in cool water to smooth, then thin down with boilin water.

Take white things, rub dirty spots on board, scrub hard, and boil, then rub colored. Don't boil just wrench and starch.

Take things out of kettle with broom stick handle, then wrench, and starch.

Hang old rags on fence. Spread tea towels on grass. Pore wrench water in flower bed. Scrub porch with hot soapy water. Turn tubs upside down.

Go put on clean dress, smooth hair with hair combs. Brew cup of tea, sit and rock a spell and count your blessings.

"I used to be lost in the shuffle.
Now I just shuffle along with the lost."

LEARN TO BE QUIET

A wise old owl sat on oak,
The more he saw, the less he spoke,
The less he spoke, the more he heard,
Why can't we be like that wise old bird?

"The greatest thing about being old is that you did not die young."

89

"Getting older is like water skiing, when you slow down, you go down."

PIONEER WOMAN

Grandmother, on a winter's day,
Milked the cows and fed them hay,
Slopped the hogs, saddled the mule
And got the children off to school;
Did the washing, mopped the floors,
Washed the windows, and did some chores;
Cooked a dish of home dried fruit,
Pressed her husband's Sunday suit,
Swept the parlor, and made a bed,
Baked a dozen loaves of bread;
Split some firewood, and lugged it in
Enough to fill the kitchen bin;
Cleaned the lamps and put in oil,
Stewed some apples she thought would spoil;
Cooked a supper that was delicious,
And afterwards washed up the dishes;
Fed the cat and sprinkled the clothes,
Mended a basketful of hose;
Then opened the organ and began to play,
"When You Come to The End Of a Perfect Day."

AN INQUISITIVE GRANDSON

One Sunday following Sunday School, a young grandson sat in the living room visiting with his grandfather. "Were you in the ark grandpa?"

"Oh no! I wasn't in the ark," replied the grandpa.

Then with a puzzled look on his face he asked, "If you weren't in the ark grandpa, how come you weren't drowned?"

BACK NEXT BIRTHDAY

A man was interviewed by a reporter on his 90th birthday. The reporter said, "I hope I can see you next year."

The man responded, "Well, son, you look healthy enough to me."

"The best thing about old age is that a person only has to go through it once."

THE 84 YEAR OLD BRIDE

The local news station was interviewing an 84 year old lady because she had just gotten married for the fourth time. The interviewer asked her questions about her life, about what it felt like to be marrying again at 84, and then about her new husband's occupation. "He's a funeral director," she answered.

"Interesting," the newsman thought. He then asked her if she wouldn't mind telling him a little about her first three husbands and what they did for a living. She paused for a few moments, needing time to reflect on all those years.

After a short time, a smile came to her face and she answered proudly, explaining that she first married a banker when she was in her early 20's, then a circus ringmaster when in her 40's, later on a preacher when in her 60's, and now, in her 80's, a funeral director.

The interviewer looked at her, quite astonished, and asked why she had married four men with such diverse careers.

"Easy son," she smiled. "I married one for the money, two for the show, three to get married, and four to go."

"If I'd known I was going to live this long, I'd have taken better care of myself." - Mickey Mantle

DO YOU REMEMBER WHEN

It took five minutes for the TV to warm up? Nearly everyone's Mom was at home when the kids got home from school? Nobody owned a purebred dog? When a quarter was a decent allowance? You'd reach into a muddy gutter for a penny? Your Mom wore nylons that came in two pieces? All your male teachers wore neckties and female teachers had their hair done every day and wore high heels? You got your windshield cleaned, oil checked, and gas pumped, without asking, all for free, every time? Laundry detergent had free glasses, dishes or towels hidden inside the box? It was considered a great privilege to be taken out to dinner at a real restaurant with your parents? They threatened to keep kids back a grade if they failed, and they did? No one ever asked where the car keys were, because they were always in the car, in the ignition, and the doors were never locked?

"You are really old if you can remember when gasoline was twenty-five cents a gallon." - A. Daniel Goldsmith

"The most telling sign of old age is not caring any more."

AGE ACTIVATED ATTENTION DEFICIT DISORDER

I decide to wash the car; I start toward the garage and notice the mail on the table. OK, I'm going to wash the car. But first I'm going to go through the mail. I lay the car keys down on the desk, discard the junk mail, and I notice the trash can is full. OK, I'll just put the bills on my desk and take the trash can out, but since I'm going to be near the mailbox anyway, I'll pay these few bills first.

Now, where is my check book? Oops, there's only one check left. My extra checks are in my desk. Oh, there's the coke I was drinking. I'm going to look for those checks. But first I need to put my coke further away from the computer, or maybe I'll pop it into the fridge to keep it cold for a while.

I head towards the kitchen and my flowers catch my eye, they need some water. I set the coke on the counter and uh-oh! There are my glasses. I was looking for them all morning! I'd better put them away first. I fill a container with water and head for the flower pots. Someone left the TV remote in the kitchen. We'll never think to look in the kitchen tonight when we want to watch television so I'd better put it back in the family room where it belongs.

I splash some water into the pots and onto the floor. I throw the remote onto a soft cushion on the sofa and I head back down the hall trying to figure out what it was I was going to do?

End of Day: The car isn't washed, the bills are unpaid, the coke is sitting on the kitchen counter, the flowers are half watered, the check book still only has one check in it and I can't seem to find my car keys! When I try to figure out how come nothing got done today, I'm baffled because I know that I was busy all day long!!

IT'S LATER THAN YOU THINK

It's later than you think! Everything is farther away now than it used to be. It's twice as far to the corner, and they've added a hill. I notice I've given up running for the bus, it leaves faster than it used to. It seems to me that they are making steps steeper than in the olden days and have you noticed the smaller print that they use in the newspapers? There is no sense asking anyone to read aloud as everyone speaks in such a low voice I can scarcely hear them. Material in dresses is so skimpy especially around the hips. It's all but impossible to reach my shoe laces. Even people are changing. They are much younger than they used to be when I was their age. On the other hand, people my age are much older than I. I ran into an old classmate the other day and she had aged so much that she didn't remember me. I got to thinking about the poor thing while I was combing my hair this morning and I glanced in the mirror at my refection and do you know, they don't make mirrors like they used to either.

"The trouble with growing old is that there's not much future in it."

"As we get older our vision should improve, not our vision of earth, but our vision of heaven." - Dr. Max Lucado

COMFORT WHILE LIVING AND WHEN DYING

It is said that when Sir Walter Scott lay dying, he said to the attendant, "Bring me the Book."

"What book?" asked the attendant.

"There is only one Book," said the dying man – "the Bible!"

Nowhere else can we find such comfort when the mists are gathering round our bed. There is no comfort in infidelity. I call the infidel to my dying bedside and say, "I'm dying. Give me something on which I can pillow my head; give me oars to steer my boat; give me something to lean on as I pass over the tide."

And the world's greatest infidel leans over my dying cot and say, "Life is a narrow veil betwixt the cold barren peaks of two eternities. We strive in vain to reach the heights. We cry aloud, and the only answer is the echo of our own dying voice."

Oh, there is no comfort in that! There is nothing there on which I can lean. Bring me the Bible and let me read, "Yea though I walk through the valley of the shadow of death, I will fear no evil; for thou art with me; thy rod and thy staff they comfort me."

Let me place my ear to this old Book and hear the immortal question of Job as it comes ringing down through the ages: "If a man dies, shall he live again?" Let me listen as the answer comes ringing back from the lips of the Son of God: "Yes! For the day shall come when the dead shall hear His voice and they that sleep in the grave shall come forth."

Oh, there is comfort in that, such comfort that I am willing to stake my life on it while living, and pillow my head upon it when I breathe my last. - Jarrette Aycock

"Nobody died when I was a child, but now it happens all the time."

AGE BEGINS TO SHOW

Bill Gaither was interviewing Eva Mae LeFevre who used to sing with her siblings in the LeFevre Trio. Bill asked Eva Mae how old she was. She replied that she was 82 years old. Bill then said to her, "You don't seem to mind telling your age."

Eva Mae responded, "Ah, no, it's just like being pregnant. Sooner or later it will begin to show."

"You're aging when your actions creak louder than your words."
- Milton Berle

THINGS YOU DON'T HEAR ANYMORE

- Be sure to refill the ice trays, we're going to have company.
- Watch for the postman, I want to get this letter to Willie in the mail today.
- Quit slamming the screen door when you go out!
- Be sure and close the windows when you leave, it looks like it's going to rain.
- Don't forget to wind the clock before you go to bed.
- Wash your feet before you go to bed. You've been playing outside barefooted.
- Why can't you remember to roll up your pant legs? Getting them caught in the bicycle chain so many times is tearing them up.
- You have torn the knees out of those pants so many times there is nothing left to put a patch on.
- Don't you go outside with your school clothes on!
- Go comb your hair. It looks like the rats have nested in it all night.
- Be sure and pour the cream off the top of the milk when you open the new bottle.
- Take that empty bottle to the store with you so you won't have to pay a deposit on another one.
- Put a dish towel over the cake so the flies won't get on it.
- Quit jumping on the floor, I have a cake in the oven and you are going to make it fall if you don't quit.
- Let me know when the Fuller brush man comes by, I need to get a few things from him.
- You boys stay close by, the car may not start and I'll need you to help push it off.
- There's a dollar in my purse. Get five gallons of gasoline when you go to town.
- Open the back door and see if you can get a breeze through here. It is getting hot.
- You can walk to the store; it won't hurt you to get some exercise.
- Don't lose that button; I'll sew it on after awhile.
- Wash your neck before you come to the table. You have beads of dirt and sweat there.
- Get out from under the sewing machine. Pumping it messes up the threads.
- Be sure to fill the lamps this morning so we won't have to do that tonight it in the dark.
- Here, take this old magazine to the toilet when you go, we are just about out of paper.
- Go out to the well and draw a bucket of water so I can wash the dishes.
- Don't turn the radio on now. I want the battery to be up when the Grand Ole Opry comes on.
- No, I don't have ten cents for you to go to the show. Do you think money grows on trees?
- Eat those turnips. They'll make you big and strong like daddy.
- That dog is not coming in the house. I don't care how cold it is, dogs don't stay in the house.
- Hush your mouth! I don't want to hear words like that or I'll wash your mouth with soap.
- It is time for your system to be cleaned out. I'm going to give you a dose of castor oil tonight.
- Sit still. I'm trying to cut your hair straight and when you keep moving it gets all messed up.
- Quit crossing your eyes, they'll get stuck that way.

94

"I learned that even when I have pains, I don't have to be one."

LOVE REQUIRES COMPROMISE

An old couple had a very happy and successful marriage. The old gentleman was once asked to what he attributed this loving relationship. "It's simple," he said, "compromise. I let her make all the small, routine decisions. She decides what house we buy, where we go on vacation, if I should change my job, and so on. I make the big, fundamental decisions. I decide if the United States should go to war or if Congress should appropriate money for a manned expedition to Mars, and so on."

OLD FOLKS ARE WORTH A FORTUNE

Old folks are worth a fortune: with silver in their hair, gold in their teeth, stones in their kidneys, lead in their feet and gas in their stomachs. I have become a lot more sociable with the passing of the years. Some might even call me a frivolous old gal. I'm seeing five gentlemen every day. As soon as I wake up Will Power helps me get out of bed. Then I go to see John. Then Charlie Horse comes along, and when he is here he takes a lot of my time and attention. When he leaves Arthur Ritis shows up and stays the rest of the day. He doesn't like to stay in one place for very long so he takes me from joint to joint. After such a busy day I'm really tired and glad to go to bed, with Ben Gay. What a life!

HEALTHY LEGACY

As we age, we usually need to work harder at maintaining our physical, emotional, and spiritual health. Here are a few important health reminders which you can apply today:

- Eat in moderation and eat a balanced diet.
- Keep your weight under control; lose weight, if necessary.
- Exercise moderately and regularly.
- Continue learning throughout life.
- Relate to younger people regularly.
- Nurture and grow your relationship with Jesus.

TOO FAST

Grandpa took his four year old grandson for a walk. The little fellow was finding it quite a problem to keep up with his grandfather's strides. "Am I walking too fast?" asked grandpa.

"No," panted the little fellow, "but I am!"

"Make it your goal to grow old gracefully and gratefully."

"When old-timers were kids they were lucky to have wall-wall-floors."

THINKING ABOUT THE HEREAFTER

The preacher came to visit the other day. He said that at my age I should be thinking about the hereafter.

I told him I do – all the time. No matter where I am, in the parlor, upstairs, in the kitchen or in the basement, I ask myself, "Now what am I here after?"

"No child is more fortunate than one with a praying parent or grandparent." - Dr. David Jeremiah

THANK YOU NOTES

One Christmas, a parent decreed that she was no longer going to remind her children of their thank-you note duties. As a result their grandmother never received acknowledgments for the generous checks she had given. The next year things were different, however.

"The children came over in person to thank me," the grandmother told a friend triumphantly.

"How wonderful!" the friend exclaimed. "What do you think caused the change in behavior?"

"Oh, that's easy," the grandmother replied. "That year I didn't sign the checks."

"You must be careful how you walk, and where you go, for there are those following you who will set their feet where yours are set."
- Dr. Robert E. Lee

HOW WILL YOU LIVE THE REST OF YOUR LIFE

The following was found in the Bible of a deceased business man in Dallas, Texas.

"I have concluded the accomplishment of wealth, even if I could achieve it, is an insufficient reason for living. When I reach the end of my days, a moment or two from now, I must look backward on something more meaningful than the pursuit of houses and land and machines and stocks and bonds. Nor is fame of any lasting benefit. I will consider my earthly existence to have been wasted unless I can recall a loving family, a consistent investment in the lives of people, and an earnest attempt to serve the God who made me. Nothing else makes much sense."

"Time may be the great healer, but it's a lousy beautician."

GRANDMA AND HER COMPUTER

The computer's swallowed grandma; yes honestly it's true,
She pressed "Control" and "Enter" and disappeared from view.
It's devoured her completely; the thought just makes me squirm.
Maybe she's caught a virus, or been eaten by a worm.
I've searched through the recycle bin and files of every kind.
I've even used the internet, but nothing did I find.
In desperation I asked Jeeves, my searches to refine.
The reply from him was negative, not a thing was found online.
So, if inside your "In Box" my grandma you should see.
Please "Scan", "Copy" and "Paste" her and e-mail her back to me.

WEIGHT PROBLEMS

We all get heavier as we get older because there's a lot more information in our heads. So I'm not fat, I'm just really intelligent and my head couldn't hold any more so it started filling up the rest of me.

GETTING OLD

Do you realize that the only time in our lives when we like to get old is when we're kids? If you're less than 10 years old, you're so excited about aging that you think in fractions. "How old are you?" "I'm four and a half!" You're never thirty-six and a half, but you're four and a half, going on five! You get into your teens, now they can't hold you back. You jump to the next number, or even a few ahead.

"How old are you?" "I'm gonna be fourteen!" You could be 13, but hey, you're gonna be 14! And then the greatest day of your life ... you become 21. Even the words sound like a ceremony ... YOU BECOME 21 ....YESSSS!!! But then you turn 30. Oooohh! What happened there? Makes you sound like bad milk. He TURNED. We had to throw him out. What's wrong? What's changed? You BECOME 21, you TURN 30, then you're PUSHING 40. Whoa! Put on the brakes, it's all slipping away. You know it. You REACH 50 and your dreams are gone!

But wait, you MAKE it to 60. You didn't think you would! So you BECOME 21, TURN 30, PUSH 40, REACH 50 and MAKE it to 60. You've built up so much speed that you HIT 70! After that it's a day by day thing. You HIT Wednesday! You get into your 80s and every day is a complete cycle. You HIT lunch. You TURN 4:30. You REACH bedtime, and it doesn't end there. Into the 90's, you start going backwards. "I was JUST 92." Then a strange thing happens. If you make it over 100, you become a little kid again. "I'm 100 and a half!" May you all make it (healthily) to 100 and a half.

"By the time you find greener pastures, you can't climb the fence."

"Just when you've learned to make the most of your life, most of your life is gone."

VALENTINE'S DAY AND SENIORS

It is that time of year again and Valentines Day has come
But now that we are seniors, some think there's no more fun

Remember those there parties that we had on Valentines Day
The teacher said "no studies now we'll spend our time with play."

We played a blind fold game where we pinned a donkey's tail
Some kids they never missed, but I always seemed to fail

It didn't matter how I tried, I couldn't pin that tail
I pinned its eyes, I pinned its legs, but never pinned its tail.

We gave each other mushy cards, "I love you," they did say
We didn't know what true love was, but we said it anyway.

We ate cup cakes and candy hearts, and had some soda pop
We had our fill and lots of fun, our teacher she was tops

But now that we are seniors, we have some different games
One we play bout everyday is called remembering names

Instead of playing hide and seek out in our school's playground
We look and look to find our keys, we're happy when they're found

We don't have races as before, like running on the track
We walk a block or maybe two, we're glad to make it back

There's hearing aids and bifocals, and don't forget the cane
These games we play bout everyday in sunshine and in rain

We still have fun on Valentines Day if seventy, eighty or more
When tired out with all this play we just lie down and snore.
- A. Daniel Goldsmith

**"My grandmother won't even buy 'green bananas!
Its an investment but it may be a bad one."**

"Laugh with people – not at them."

"Few men run well to the end." - L.E. Maxwell

JUST A MINUTE

I have only just a minute, just sixty seconds in it;
Forced upon me, can't refuse it, didn't seek it, didn't choose it;
I must suffer if I lose it, give account if I abuse it;
Just a tiny little minute, but eternity is in it.

NO WRINKLES ON THE SOUL

My hands are trembling,
My feet are slipping,
My back is aching,
But there's not a wrinkle on my soul.

My eyes are squinting,
My ears are failing,
My mind is groping,
But there's not a wrinkle on my soul.

My things I'm dropping,
My years are fleeting,
My friends are dying,
But there's not a wrinkle on my soul.

I've a faith that's unwavering,
I've a hope that's persisting,
I've a love that's enduring,
There's not a wrinkle on my soul.

I've a joy that's unending,
I've a peace that's long lasting,
I've friends that are most caring,
There's not a wrinkle on my soul.

Yes, my body it is aging,
But my spirit is rejoicing,
For my God He is so loving,
There's not a wrinkle on my soul.
- A. Daniel Goldsmith

"When I was younger, I could remember anything, whether it happened or not." - Mark Twain

"No one can go back and make a brand new start. Anyone can start from now and make a brand new ending."

I AIN'T DEAD YET

My hair is white and I'm almost blind,
The days of my youth are far behind,
My neck's so stiff, can't turn my head,
Can't hear half that's being said.
My legs are wobbly, can hardly walk,
But glory be, I can surely talk.
And this is the message I want you to get:
I'm still a-kickin', and I ain't dead yet.

My joints are stiff, won't move in their sockets,
And nary a dime is left in my pockets,
But still I have just loads of fun
And my heart with joy is overrun.
I've lots of friends, so kind and sweet,
And many more I never meet.
Oh, this is a wonderful world of ours,
Shade and sunshine and beautiful flowers.
So you just take it from me, you bet,
I'm glad I'm living, and I ain't dead yet.

I've got corns on my feet and ingrown nails,
And do they hurt? Here language fails;
To tell you my troubles would take too long,
If I tried, you sure would give me the gong.
I go to church and Sunday school, too,
For I love the story that is ever new.
And when I reach the end of my row,
I hope to my heavenly home I'll go;
Then when I leave my house of clay,
If you listen closely, I'm apt to say,
"Well, folks, I've left you, but don't forget,
I've just passed on, but I ain't dead yet!"
                    - Written by a 94 year old lady

"To be seventy years young is sometimes far more cheerful and hopeful than to be forty years old."
                    - Oliver Holmes

"Nothing ages a man faster than trying to prove he's still young."

SECRET TO LONGEVITY

When a man reached his 100th birthday, a local news reporter interviewed him. "What's your secret to longevity?" asked the reporter.

"I never argue," said the century old man.

"Surely that can't be it," said the reporter.

The man shrugged his shoulders, "I suppose you're right."

IT PAYS TO ADVERTISE

Grandpa was a skilled CPA who was not great at self-promotion. He was a good accountant but reluctant to put himself forward. So when an advertising company offered to put grandpa's business placard in the shopping carts of a supermarket, he jumped at the chance. A full year went by before he got the first call that could be traced to the shopping cart placard.

"Is this Richard Larson, CPA?" the caller asked.

"That's right," grandpa answered. "May I help you?"

"Yes," the caller said, "one of your shopping carts is in my yard, and I want you to come and get it."

"If growing old catches you by surprise, don't blame God. He gave you plenty of warning. He also gave you plenty of advice."
- Dr. Max Lucado

PARTING WORDS

A pastor was leaving his area and was saying farewell to his congregation at the church doors for the last time. He shook the hand of an elderly lady as she walked out. She said "Your successor won't be as good as you."

"Nonsense," said the pastor in a flattered tone.

"No, really," said the lady, "I've been here under five different ministers and each new one has been worse than the previous one."

"If you are too busy to laugh, you're entirely too busy."

HYMNS vs CHORUSES

An old farmer went to the city one weekend and attended the big city church. He came home and his wife asked him how it was.

"Well," said the farmer, "It was good. They did something different, however. They sang praise choruses instead of hymns."

"Praise choruses?" said his wife. "What are those?"

"Oh, they're OK. They are sort of like hymns, only different," said the farmer.

"Well, what's the difference?" asked his wife.

The farmer said, "Well, it's like this – If I were to say to you: 'Martha, the cows are in the corn' – well, that would be a hymn. If on the other hand, I were to say to you:

> Martha, Martha, Martha,
> Oh Martha, Martha, Martha,
> The cows, the big cows, the brown cows,
> The black cows, the white cows,
> The cows, cows, cows
> Are in the corn
> Are in the corn, are in the corn, are in the corn,
> The corn, corn, corn.'

Then, if I were to repeat the whole thing two or three times, well, that would be a praise chorus."

The next weekend, his nephew, a young, new Christian from the city came to visit and attended the small town local church, his aunt and uncle's church. He went home and his mother asked him how it was.

"Well," said the young man, "It was good. They did something different however. They sang hymns instead of regular songs."

"Hymns?" asked his mother. "What are those?"

"Oh, they're OK. They are sort of like regular songs, only different," said the young man.

"Well, what's the difference?" asked his mother.

The young man said, "Well, it's like this – If I were to say to you: 'Martha, the cows are in the corn' – well, that would be a regular song. If on the other hand, I were to say to you:

Oh Martha, dear Martha, hear thou my cry
Inclinest thine ear to the words of my mouth
Turn thou thy whole wondrous ear by and by
To the righteous, inimitable, glorious truth.

For the way of the animals who can explain
There in their heads is no shadow of sense
Hearkenest they in God's sun or His rain
Unless from the mild, tempting corn they are fenced.

Yea those cows in glad bovine, rebellious delight
Have broke free their shackles, their warm pens eschewed
Then goaded by minions of darkness and night
They all my mild tender sweet corn they have chewed.

So look to the bright shining day by and by
Where all foul corruptions of earth are reborn
Where no vicious animals make my soul cry
And I no longer see those foul cows in the corn.

Then if I were to do only verses one, three and four and do a key change on the last verse, well that would be a hymn.

"You're getting old when you get the same sensation from a rocking chair that you once got from a roller coaster."

DRESSING UP FOR THEIR 40th ANNIVERSARY

John and Nancy were married for 40 years and decided they wanted to renew their vows and planned a second wedding. They were discussing the details with their friends. Nancy wasn't going to wear a traditional bridal gown and she started describing the dress she was planning to wear. One of her friends asked what color shoes she had to go with the dress.

Nancy replied, "Silver."

At that point, her husband chimed in, "Yep silver to match her hair."

Shooting a glaring look at John's bald spot Nancy's friend said, "So, John, I guess you are going barefoot."

"Old age is when you're willing to get up and give your seat to a lady, but you can't."

"It's not how long you live that counts, but how you live."

A LITTLE BIT FISHY

Grandpa was a family doctor, and also an avid fisherman. One day while he was on one of his frequent fishing trips, he got a call that a woman at a neighboring farm was giving birth. He rushed to her aid and delivered a healthy baby boy. The farmer had nothing to weigh the baby with so the doctor used his fishing scales. The baby weighed 32 pounds and 10 ounces.

THEY FOUND THE PERFECT CHURCH

My next door neighbors, who recently retired, moved to another city to be near their children and grandchildren. They wrote and told us that they had found the perfect church. They told us that this new church that they were attending has four worship services each Sunday.

There was one for those new to the faith; another for those who liked traditional worship; one for those who'd lost their faith and would like to get it back, and another for those who had bad experiences with churches and were complaining about it.

They have names for each of the services: FINDERS, KEEPERS, LOSERS, WEEPERS

HE LIVETH

He liveth long who liveth well, all other life is short and vain;
He liveth longest who can tell, of living most for heavenly gain.
- Horatius Bonar

"The best way to prevent your body from sagging, is to eat until the wrinkles all fill out."

HAVING A LITTLE FUN

I went to the store the other day. I was only in there for about 5 minutes. When I came out there was a city cop writing out a parking ticket. I went up to him and said, "Come on, Buddy, how about giving a senior a break." He ignored me and continued writing the ticket. I called him a name. He glared at me and started writing another ticket for having worn tires. So I called him a worse name. He finished the second ticket and put it on the windshield with the first.

Then he started writing a third ticket. This went on for about 20 minutes. The more I abused him, the more tickets he wrote. I didn't care. My car was parked around the corner. I try to have a little fun each day now that I'm retired.

"Middle age is when you go all out and end up all in."

104

BEAUTY MARKS

An elderly woman and her little grandson, whose face was sprinkled with bright freckles, spent the day at the zoo. Lots of children were waiting in line to get their cheeks painted by a local artist who was decorating them with tiger paws.

"You've got so many freckles, there's no place to paint!" a girl in the line said to the little fella. Embarrassed, the little boy dropped his head.

His grandmother knelt down next to him. "I love your freckles. When I was a little girl I always wanted freckles," she said, while tracing her finger across the child's cheek. "Freckles are beautiful!"

The boy looked up, "Really?"

"Of course," said the grandmother. "Why just name me one thing that's more beautiful than freckles."

The little boy thought for a moment, peered intensely into his grandma's face, and softly whispered, "Wrinkles."

THE USHER

An elderly woman walked into the local country church. The friendly usher greeted her at the door and helped her up the flight of steps, "Where would you like to sit?" he asked politely.

"The front row please," she answered.

"You really don't want to do that," the usher said. "The pastor is really boring."

"Do you happen to know who I am?" the woman inquired.

"No," he said.

"I'm the pastor's mother," she replied indignantly.

"Do you know who I am?" he asked.

"No." she said.

"Good," he answered.

"Retirement for some people is having nothing to do and all day to do it in."

**"I knew I was going bald when
it was taking longer and longer to wash my face."**

THE OUTHOUSE

An old-timer told about the time when he was a teenager and wrote to Sears to order some toilet tissue for the outhouse. Sears sent the toilet tissue, but accompanying the order was a note requesting that the next time he ordered to order from the catalog, with the catalog number, etc. The old-timer wrote back to Sears and said, "If I had had your catalog, I would not have had to order any toilet tissue."

YES, I'M A SENIOR CITIZEN

I'm the life of the party...even if it lasts until 8 p.m.
I'm very good at opening child proof caps with a hammer.
I'm usually interested in going home before I get to where I am going.
I'm awake many hours before my body allows me to get up.
I'm smiling all the time because I can't hear a thing you're saying.
I'm very good at telling stories; over and over and over and over...
I'm aware that other people's grandchildren are not as cute as mine.
I'm so cared for -- long term care, eye care, private care, dental care.
I'm not grouchy; I just don't like traffic, waiting, crowds, politicians.
I'm sure everything I can't find is in a secure place.
I'm wrinkled, saggy, lumpy, and that's just my left leg.
I'm having trouble remembering simple words like...
I'm realizing that aging is not for wimps.
I'm sure they are making adults much younger these days, and when did they let kids become policemen.
I'm wondering, if you're only as old as you feel, how could I be alive at 150?
I'm a walking storeroom of facts ... I've just lost the key to the storeroom door.
Yes, I'm a SENIOR CITIZEN and I think I am having the time of my life!

A WALKING ECONOMY

Sitting in McDonalds and enjoying a coffee, a senior said to his friend, "I'm a walking economy."

The friend asked, "How's that?"

"Well," he said, "My hair line is in recession, my stomach is a victim of inflation, and both of these together are putting me into a deep depression!"

**"Old age, as an abstraction, never arrives.
Like a balloon, it stays comfortably ahead of us."**

WHERE IS MY PAPER

The irate senior calling the newspaper office, loudly demanded to know where her Sunday edition of the newspaper was. "Ma'am," said the employee, today is Saturday. The Sunday paper is not delivered until Sunday.

There was quite a pause on the other end of the phone, followed by a ray of recognition. "So that's why no one was at church today."

EMPATHY

While I sat in the reception area of my doctor's office, a woman rolled an elderly man in a wheelchair into the room. As she went to the receptionist's desk, the man sat there, alone and silent. Just as I was thinking I should make small talk with him, a little boy slipped off his mother's lap and walked over to the wheelchair. Placing his hand on the man's, he said, "I know how you feel. My mom makes me ride in the stroller too."

TRUE LOVE

It was a busy morning, about 8:30, when an elderly gentleman in his 80's arrived to have stitches removed from his thumb. He said he was in a hurry as he had an appointment at 9:00 am. I took his vital signs and had him take a seat, knowing it would be over an hour before someone would to able to see him. I saw him looking at his watch and decided, since I was not busy with another patient, I would evaluate his wound. On exam, it was well healed, so I talked to one of the doctors, got the needed supplies to remove his sutures and redress his wound.

While taking care of his wound, I asked him if he had another doctor's appointment this morning, as he was in such a hurry. The gentleman told me no, that he needed to go to the nursing home to eat breakfast with his wife. I inquired as to her health. He told me that she had been there for a while and that she was a victim of Alzheimer's disease.

As we talked, I asked if she would be upset if he was a bit late. He replied that she no longer knew who he was, that she had not recognized him in five years now. I was surprised, and asked him, "And you still go every morning, even though she doesn't know who you are?"

He smiled as he patted my hand and said, "She doesn't know me, but I still know who she is." I had to hold back tears as he left, I had goose bumps on my arm, and thought, that is the kind of love I want in my life.

True love is neither physical, nor romantic. True love is an acceptance of all that is, has been, will be, and will not be. The happiest people don't necessarily have the best of everything; they just make the best of everything they have.

"As we face troubled waters it is not to drown us, but to cleanse us."

AN UNDERSTANDING GRANDAUGHTER

Out bicycling one day with my eight-year-old granddaughter, Carolyn, I got a little wistful. "In ten years," I said, "you'll want to be with your friends and you won't go walking, biking, and swimming with me like you do now."

Carolyn shrugged. "In ten years you'll be too old to do all those things anyway."

THE SECRET TO GETTING RICH

A young man asked an old rich man, who was 99 years old, how he made his money. The old guy fingered his worsted wool vest and said, "Well, son, it was 1932, the depth of the Great Depression. I was down to my last nickel. I invested that nickel in an apple. I spent the entire day polishing the apple and, at the end of the day, I sold the apple for ten cents.

The next morning, I invested those ten cents in two apples. I spent the entire day polishing them and sold them at 5:00pm for 20 cents.

I continued this system for a week, by the end of which I'd accumulated a fortune of $3.20. Then my wife's father died and left us ten million dollars."

I LOVE TO SING HYMNS

I love to sing the hymns of old
The sweetest story ever told,
My sins are blotted out I know
O love that wilt not let me go.

Amazing grace how sweet the sound
Lord plant my feet on higher ground.
All praise to Him who reigns above
Are you, are you washed in the blood?

And can it be that I should gain
I love to sing, Jesus shall reign;
Beyond the sunset, face to face
It's all because redeeming grace.

The old rugged cross, a favorite hymn
He's coming soon, praise Him, praise Him
He'll understand and say well done,
I love those hymns, yes everyone.
- A. Daniel Goldsmith

"Stories from the past can give us pointers for the present."

I'M A PACK RAT

Every New Year I start stirring in my stuff. There is closet stuff, drawer stuff, attic stuff and basement stuff. I separate the good stuff from the bad stuff and then I put the bad stuff anywhere that is not too crowded, until I decide if I will need the bad stuff again.

Sometimes visitors come and bring bags and bags of stuff, so we move our stuff to make room for their stuff. It would be so much easier if they would just use some of our stuff and leave their stuff at home with the rest of their stuff.

This Fall I had an extra closet built so I would have a place for all the stuff too good to throw away and too bad to keep with my good stuff. Now you may not have this problem, but I seem to spend a lot of time with stuff! Food stuff, cleaning stuff, medicine stuff, clothes stuff and outside stuff; stuff to make us look younger, stuff to make us look healthier, stuff to hold us in and stuff to fill us out, stuff to read, stuff to entertain us, and stuff to eat, so we stuff ourselves with the food stuff.

When the Lord calls me Home, my children will want the good stuff, but the bad stuff will be stuffed in bags and taken to the dump where all the other people's stuff has been stuffed.

Here on earth our lives are so filled with stuff; good stuff, bad stuff, little stuff, big stuff, useful stuff, junky stuff, and everyone's stuff. Now, when we leave our stuff and go to heaven, whatever happens to our stuff won't really matter. We shall have all the good, Heavenly stuff God has prepared for us. NO BAD STUFF THERE!

"I've learned one thing in life, if you do it right the first time, you don't have to do it again." - Dr. John MacArthur

WHAT ARE GRANDMAS

Grandmas are moms with lots of frosting.
Grandmas are just "antique" little girls.
Grandmas are babysitters who watch the kids instead of the television.
Grandmas never run out of hugs or cookies.
Grandmas hold our tiny hands for just a little while, but our hearts forever.
Grandmas are wonderful mothers with lots of practice.
Grandmas are short on criticism and long on love.

**"Laughter is the cheapest luxury that man has.
It stirs up the blood, expands the chest, electrifies the nerves,
clears the cobwebs out of the brain and
gives the whole system a cleansing."**

"A man with a sense of humor doesn't make jokes out of life; he merely recognizes the ones that are there."

HANGING WALLPAPER

My father, who is retired and living in a condominium, decided to redecorate his bedroom. He wasn't sure how many rolls of wallpaper he would need, but he knew that his friend next door had recently done the same job and the two rooms were identical in size.

"Henry," he said, "how many rolls of wallpaper did you buy for your bedroom?"

"Ten," said George.

So dad bought ten rolls of paper and did the job, but he had two rolls left over.

"George," he said, "I bought ten rolls of wallpaper for the bedroom, but I've got two rolls left over!"

"Yeah," said George. "So did I."

"Humor is the hole that lets the sawdust out of a stuffed shirt."

I KNOW WHO YOU ARE

When grandma and I were out for dinner the other day, we ordered off of the senior's menu. It seemed like forever, and we still hadn't received our food. I was getting a little impatient and hollered to the waitress. "Waitress, have you forgotten me?"

She answered quickly, and politely, "Oh, no, sir. Indeed not. You're the stuffed tomato."

VERY OBSERVANT

A woman was preparing dinner, for several members of her family. Her youngest grand-daughter was following her around in the kitchen. The grand-daughter eventually asked permission to help by putting the silverware in place. Grandma was pleased with the offer of help. Later, when the family had been called to the table and all were seated, grandma looked up in surprise and exclaimed. "Why, Susie, you didn't give Uncle Pete a knife and fork."

Susie replied, "I didn't think that he would need any. Daddy said that Uncle Pete eats like a horse."

"The trouble in marriage often starts when the man is so busy earning his salt that he forgets his honey."

A PROBLEM

Our elderly neighbor has an identity problem and an energy crisis. He doesn't know who he is and he is too tired to find out.

THE PASTOR PHONED

A grandmother was trying hard to get the ketchup to come out of the bottle. During her struggle the telephone rang so she asked her four-year old grand-daughter to answer the phone. "It's the pastor, Grandma," the child said to her grand-mother. Then the grand-daughter continued her conversation with the pastor and said, "Grandma can't come to the phone right now. She's hitting the bottle."

"If we are impatient, unkind and unforgiving now, we won't wake up at 65 to discover people want to be around us." - Nettie McKenzie

GENEALOGY QUESTION

When my granddaughter, Mary, was 9-years-old, she was given an assignment by her teacher to write a story on "Where my family came from." The purpose was to understand your genealogy.

I was not aware of her assignment when she asked me at the dining room table one night, "Grandma, where did I come from?"

I responded quite nervously because my son and daughter-in-law were out of town and I was stalling until they returned home, "Well, honey, the stork brought you."

"Where did Mom come from then?"

"The stork brought her too."

"OK, then where did you come from?"

"The stork brought me too, dear."

"Okay, thanks, Grandma."

I did not think anything more about it until two days later when I was cleaning Mary's room and read the first sentence of her paper, "For three generations there have been no natural births in our family."

"You may soon forget those with whom you have laughed, but you will never forget those with whom you have wept."

"What you will be tomorrow depends on the choices you make today."

BURMA SHAVE SIGNS

Before the US Interstates existed, Burma Shave signs dotted the farmers' fields along the old two lane roads. Five small red signs with white letters, about 100 feet apart, each one containing one line of a four line couplet. The fifth sign advertised Burma Shave, a popular shaving cream. Many of these signs served as a reminder to drive safely. Here are a few of those unique safety signs.

DON'T LOSE YOUR HEAD
TO GAIN A MINUTE
YOU NEED YOUR HEAD
YOUR BRAINS ARE IN IT

DROVE TOO LONG
DRIVER SNOOZING
WHAT HAPPENED NEXT
IS NOT AMUSING

BROTHER SPEEDER,
LET'S REHEARSE;
ALL TOGETHER,
GOOD MORNING NURSE

SPEED WAS HIGH
WEATHER WAS NOT
TIRES WERE THIN
X MARKS THE SPOT

AROUND THE CURVE
LICKETY-SPLIT
IT'S A BEAUTIFUL NEW CAR
WASN'T IT?

NO MATTER THE PRICE
NO MATTER HOW NEW
THE BEST SAFETY DEVICE
IN THE CAR IS YOU

A GUY WHO DRIVES
A CAR WIDE OPEN
IS NOT THINKIN'
HE'S JUST HOPIN'

AT INTERSECTIONS
LOOK EACH WAY
A HARP SOUNDS NICE
BUT ITS HARD TO PLAY

BOTH HANDS ON THE WHEEL
EYES ON THE ROAD
THAT'S THE SKILLFUL
DRIVER'S CODE

CAR IN DITCH
DRIVER IN TREE
THE MOON WAS FULL
AND SO WAS HE.

PASSING SCHOOL ZONE
TAKE IT SLOW
LET OUR LITTLE
SHAVERS GROW

DON'T STICK YOUR ELBOW
OUT TOO FAR
IT MIGHT GO HOME
IN ANOTHER CAR.

HER CHARIOT RACED
AT 90 PER
THEY HAULED AWAY
WHAT HAD BEN HUR

DO NOT PASS
ON CURVE OR HILL
IF THE COPS DON'T CATCH YOU
THE MORTICIANS WILL

HE SAW THE TRAIN
HE TRIED TO DUCK IT
KICKED FIRST THE GAS
AND THEN THE BUCKET

DON'T TRY PASSING
ON A SLOPE
UNLESS YOU HAVE
A PERISCOPE

A DIFFERENT DAY AND AGE

"Hey Papa," one of my grandsons asked the other day, "What was your favorite fast food when you were growing up?"

"We didn't have fast food when I was growing up," I informed him. "All the food was slow."

"C'mon, seriously. Where did you eat?"

"It was a place called 'at home'," I explained. "My mother, your great grandma cooked every day and when my Dad got home from work, we sat down together at the dining room table, and if I didn't like what she put on my plate I was allowed to sit there until I did like it."

By this time, my grandson was laughing so hard I was afraid he was going to suffer serious internal damage, so I didn't tell him the part about how I had to have permission to leave the table.

But here are some other things I would have told him about my childhood if I figured his system could have handled it:

Some parents NEVER owned their own house, wore Levis, set foot on a golf course, traveled out of the country or had a credit card. In their later years they had something called a revolving charge card. The card was good only at Sears.

My parents never drove me to soccer practice. This was mostly because we never had heard of soccer. I had a bicycle that weighed probably 50 pounds, and only had one speed, (slow). We didn't have a television in our house until I was 11, but my grandparents had one before that. It was, of course, black and white, but they bought a piece of colored plastic to cover the screen. The top third was blue, like the sky, and the bottom third was green, like grass. The middle third was red. It was perfect for programs that had scenes of fire trucks riding across someone's lawn on a sunny day. Some people had a lens taped to the front of the TV to make the picture look larger.

I was 13 before I tasted my first pizza and it was called "pizza pie." When I bit into it, I burned the roof of my mouth and the cheese slid off, swung down, plastered itself against my chin and burned that, too. It's still the best pizza I ever had.

We didn't have a car until I was 15. Before that, the only car in our family was my grandfather's Ford. He called it a "machine."

I never had a telephone in my room. The only phone in the house was in the living room and it was on a party line. Before you could dial, you had to listen and make sure some people you didn't know weren't already using the line.

Pizzas were not delivered to our home, but milk was. All newspapers were delivered by boys and all boys delivered newspapers. I delivered a newspaper, six days a week. It cost 7 cents a paper, of which I got to keep 2 cents. I had to get up at 4 AM every morning. On Saturday, I had to collect the 42 cents from my customers. My favorite customers were the ones who gave me 50 cents and told me to keep the change. My least favorite customers were the ones who seemed to never be home on collection day. Growing up isn't what it used to be.

**"The pursuit of happiness is the chase of a lifetime!
It is never too late to become what I might have been."**

NEEDED SOME ADVICE

An enormously wealthy 65-year-old man falls in love with a young woman in her twenties and is contemplating a proposal. "Do you think she'd marry me if I tell her I'm 45?" he asked a friend.

"With your wealth, your chances would be much better," said the friend, "if you tell her you're 90."

**"I was always taught to respect my elders,
but it keeps getting harder to find one."**

LISTEN TO THE SERMON

During a sermon one Sunday, the pastor saw two teenage girls who were sitting near the back of the sanctuary, giggling and disturbing people.

He interrupted his sermon and announced sternly, "There are two of you here who have not heard a word I've said." That quieted them down.

When the service was over, he went to the door to greet the parishioners. Three different senior adults apologized for going to sleep in church, promising it would never happen again.

**"I don't feel old; in fact I don't feel anything until noon,
then it's time for my nap."** - Bob Hope

HOW MANY DO YOU REMEMBER

Head light's dimmer switches on the floor.
Ignition switches on the dashboard.
Heaters mounted on the inside of the fire wall.
Real ice boxes.
Pant leg clips for bicycles without chain guards.
Using hand signals for cars without turn signals.

FINAL EXAMS

Two little girls were discussing their families. "Why does your grandmother read the Bible so much?" she asked.

"I think," said the other girl, "that's she's cramming for her finals."

**"You can tell when you're getting old.
Your feet hurt even before you get out of bed."**

SENIOR TRAVELERS

A travel agent looked up from his desk to see an old lady and an old gentleman peering in the shop window at the posters showing the glamorous destinations around the world. The agent had a good week and the dejected couple looking in the window gave him a rare feeling of generosity. He called them into his shop: "I know that on your pension you could never hope to have a holiday, so I am sending you off to a fabulous resort at my expense, and I won't take no for an answer"

He took them inside and asked his secretary to write two flight tickets and book a room in a five star hotel. They, as can be expected, gladly accepted, and were off! About a month later the little old lady came in to his shop. "And how did you like your holiday?" he asked eagerly. "The flight was exciting and the room was lovely," she said. "I've come to thank you but, one thing puzzled me. Who was that old guy I had to share the room with?"

Actually, some wives ask the same question every morning!

**"Life is a journey, not a guided tour. So don't miss the ride.
Have a great time going around. You don't get a second shot at it."**

A WONDERFUL EXPLANATION

A sick man turned to his doctor, as he was preparing to leave the examination room and said, "Doctor, I am afraid to die. Tell me what lies on the other side."

Very quietly, the doctor said, "I don't know."

"You don't know? You, a Christian man, do not know what is on the other side?"

The doctor was holding the handle of the door. On the other side came a sound of scratching and whining, and as he opened the door, a dog sprang into the room and leaped on him with an eager show of gladness.

Turning to the patient, the doctor said, "Did you notice my dog? He's never been in this room before. He didn't know what was inside. He knew nothing except that his master was here, and when the door opened, he sprang in without fear. I know little of what is on the other side of death, but I do know one thing... I know my Master is there and that is enough."

**"To live above with saints we love, that will be glory.
To live below with saints we know, well that's another story."**

A SOLDIER SENDS LETTER HOME

I'm one of these fellows trying to make the world safe for democracy. I fought and fought, but I had to go anyway. I was in Class A. The next time I want to be in Class B: B here when they leave, and B here when they come back. I remember when I registered. I went up to the desk and the, man in charge was my milkman. He said, "What is your name?" I said, "Oh, you know me." "What's your name?" he barked. I told him, "August Childes."

He said, "Are you alien?" I said, "No, I feel fine." He asked me where I was born and I said, Pittsburgh. He then said, "When did you first see the light of day?" I said, "When we moved to Philadelphia." He asked me how old I was, so I told him, twenty-three the first day of September. He said, "The first day of September you will be in China and that will be the last of August."

Then I went to camp and I guess they didn't think I would live long. The first fellow I saw wrote on my card "Flying Corpse." I went along a little farther and some fellow said, "Look at what the wind blew in." I said, "Wind nothin' the draft is doing it." On the second morning they put these clothes on me. What an outfit. As soon as you're in it, you think you could fight anybody. They have two sizes, too small and too big. The pants were so tight I couldn't sit down. The shoes were so big I turned around three times and they didn't move. What a raincoat they gave me. It strained the rain. I passed an officer all dressed up with a belt and all that stuff. He said. "Didn't you notice my uniform when you passed?" I said, "yeah, but what are you kicking about? Look at what they gave me."

One morning when it was about 50 below, they called us out for underwear inspection. Talk about scenery! The union suit I had on would fit Tony Galento. The Lieutenant lined us up and told us to stand up. He looked at me and I told him, "I am up sir, but this underwear I have on makes you think I'm sitting down." He got so mad he put me out digging a ditch. A little later he passed me and said, don't throw the dirt up there. I asked him where am I going to put it? He said to dig another hole and put it there.

Three days later we sailed for The Philippines. Marching down the pier I had the worst luck. I had a sergeant who stuttered and it took him so long to say halt that 21 of us marched overboard. They pulled us out and lined us up on the pier. The captain said, "Fall in." I said, "I've been in sir."

Well, we landed and were immediately sent to the trenches. After two nights the cannons began to roar and the shells started to pop. I was shaking with patriotism. I tried to hide behind a tree but there weren't enough trees for the officers. The captain came around and said, "We're going over the top at five o'clock." I said, "I'd like to have a furlough." He said, "Have you any red blood in you?" I said, "Yes, but I don't want to see it."

Five o'clock and we went over the top and 10,000 of the enemy soldiers came at us and they looked at me as if I had started the war. Our captain said, "Fire at will." But I didn't know anybody by that name. I guess the fellow behind thought I was Will, for he fired and shot me.

Bye for now.

"Smile and the world smiles with you. Snore and you sleep alone."

SENIOR'S MENU WHEN FLYING

A senior citizen in Indiana said, "I guess I'm getting old. I took my first airplane flight yesterday and the stewardess asked if I wanted coffee, tea, or Geritol."

**"If you see a man who always agrees with you, watch him,
he is apt to lie about other things too."** - Dr. Robert A. Cook

A RETIRED PASTOR

A retired pastor decided to join a community service club. The members of the club thought that they would have some fun with this pastor. So under his name on the badge they printed: "Hog caller" as his occupation.

Everyone made a big fanfare as the badge was presented. The pastor responded by saying: "Over the years, as a pastor, I was usually called Shepherd of the sheep, but then you know your people better than I do."

"Dieting is when you starve yourself to death so you can live longer."

LIFE LONG LEARNING

Learn to laugh – it's better than medicine.
Learn the art of saying kind things – it makes everyone feel better, including you.
Learn not to be over critical – critics are a dime a dozen.
Learn to keep your troubles to yourself – everyone has them and no one wants to hear yours.
Learn to listen – you'll be surprised at what you don't know.
Learn to greet everyone with a smile – you may save someone's day.
Learn to forgive – forgiveness brings peace and healing inside.

SILENCE BROKEN

A retired couple often had their disagreements. After one heated argument, the husband took his wife for a car ride. He thought maybe the ride would ease the tensions. They drove for several miles, neither of them saying one word. Finally, as they passed a farm with several mules, goats, and pigs, the husband asked sarcastically, "Relatives of yours?"

"Yep," the wife replied, "in-laws!"

**"God loves everyone, but prefers
'fruit of the spirit' over 'religious nuts'!"**

WISDOM OF SOLOMON

Several women appeared in court, each accusing the other of the trouble in their apartments. They all lived on the same floor. The judge, with the wisdom of Solomon, called for an orderly testimony. "I'll hear the oldest first," he decreed. The case was closed for lack of evidence.

"When I was a boy my hair was light, then it turned dark, then it turned grey, then it turned loose."

HOW OLD DO I LOOK

My wife bought a new line of expensive cosmetics guaranteed to make her look years younger. After a lengthy sitting before the mirror applying the "miracle" products, she asked, "Darling, honestly, what age would you say I am?"

Looking over her carefully, I replied, "Judging from your skin, twenty; your hair, eighteen; and your figure, twenty-five."

"Oh, you flatterer!" she gushed.

"Hey, wait a minute!" I interrupted, "I haven't added them up yet."

HOSPITAL RULES

While working as a student nurse, I found one elderly gentleman, already dressed and sitting on the bed with a suitcase at his feet. He insisted that he didn't need my help to leave the hospital. After a chat about rules being rules, and that he needed to use the wheel chair, he reluctantly let me wheel him to the elevator. On the way down I asked him if his wife was meeting him. "I don't know," he said. "She's still upstairs in the bathroom changing out of her hospital gown."

A LITTLE BOY IN EACH OLD MAN

A distinguished elderly gentleman, walking through the toy department, stopped to admire a toy train. It whistled, belched smoke, deposited milk cans, in fact did virtually everything a real freight train does. After looking at it for some time he finally said, "I'll take it. Please have it wrapped."

The clerk said, "Fine, I'm sure your grandson will love it."

The elderly gentleman said thoughtfully, "That's right. Maybe you'd better give me two of them."

"Seniors with good old fashioned horse sense know when to say "nay."

119

TOMBSTONE EPITAPHS

Round Rock, Texas
"I told you I was sick."

London, England - Ann Mann
"Here lies Ann Mann, who lived an old maid but died an old Mann"

Dalhousie, Nova Scotia – Ezekial Aikle
"Here lies Ezekial Aikle, age 102. The Good die young"

Ruidoso, New Mexico – Johnny Yeast
"Here lies Johnny Yeast, pardon me for not rising"

Hatfield, Massachusetts – Arabella Young
"Beneath this stone, a lump of clay, lies Arabella Young
Who on the 21st of May began to hold her tongue."

Uniontown, Pennsylvania – Jonathan Blake
"Here lies the body of Jonathan Blake
Stepped on the gas instead of the brake."

Nantucket, Massachusetts – Jonathan Pease
"Under the sod and under the trees, lies the body of Jonathan Pease.
He is not here, there's only the pod, Pease shelled out and went to God."

Thurmont, Maryland
"Here lies an Atheist, all dressed up, and no place to go."

Wimborne, England –John Penny
"Reader if cash thou art, in want of any
Dig four feet deep and thou wilt find a Penny."

Richmond, Virginia – Margaret Daniels
"She always said her feet were killing her but nobody believed her."

In a cemetery in England:
"Remember man, as you walk by.
As you are now, so once was I.
As I am now, so shall you be.
Remember this and follow me."
To which someone replied by writing on the tombstone:
"To follow you I'm not content.
Until I know which way you went."

Hartscombe, England – Jonathan Fiddle
"On the 22nd of June Jonathan Fiddle went out of tune"

Niagara Falls, Ontario – Ephraim Wise
"Here lies the body of Ephraim Wise, safely tucked between his two wives.
One was Tillie and the other Sue, both were faithful, loyal, and true.
By his request in ground that's hilly, his coffin is tilted toward Tillie."

Albany, New York – Harry Edsel Smith
"Looked up the elevator shaft to see if the car was on the way down. It was."

England – Sir John Strange
"Here lies an honest lawyer, and that is Strange."

London, England – Owen Moore
"Gone away, owin' more, than he could pay."

Edinburgh, Scotland – Dentist Brown
"Stranger, tread this ground with gravity, Dentist Brown is filling his last cavity."

Enosburg Falls, Vermont – Anna Hopewell
"Here lies the body of our Anna, done to death by a banana,
It wasn't the fruit that laid her low, but the skin of the thing that made her go."

Charlotte, North Carolina – Ruth Bell Graham
"End of Construction – Thank you for your patience."

Abbotsford, British Columbia – Harry Harms, a letter carrier
"Return to Sender – Postage paid in full by the blood of Christ."

Apple Valley, California – Roy Rogers
The Cowboy's Prayer
"Oh Lord, I reckon I'm not much just by myself.
I fail to do a lot of things I ought to do.
But Lord, when trails are steep and passes high,
Help me to ride it straight the whole way through.
And when in the falling dusk I get the final call,
I do not care how many flowers they send—
Above all else the happiest trail would be
For You to say to me, 'Let's ride, My friend.' Amen."

Olney, England – John Newton
John Newton, Clerk, once an infidel and libertine, a servant of slaves in Africa, was
by the rich mercy of our Lord and Savior Jesus Christ, preserved, restored, pardoned, and
appointed to preach the faith he had long labored to destroy

JUST MARRIED

A bride bent with age, leaned over her cane,
Her steps uncertain need guiding.
While down the church aisle with a long toothless smile
The groom in a wheel chair gliding.
And who is this elderly couple thus wed
You'll find when you closely explore it
This is that rare most conservative pair
Who waited till they could afford it.

A FUNERAL FOR THE BIRDS

An elderly lady phoned a Baptist preacher to come and perform the funeral for the woman's pet canary. "Oh, madam, we can't do that here but if you call Rev. John Jones, down the street, I am sure that he will be able to assist you."

"Well, that's fine," said the woman. "By the way, I hate to ask the other pastor, but I was wondering if you think a fee of $2,000.00 would cover the expenses?"

"Madam, why didn't you tell me it was a Baptist canary?"

"Swallowing your pride will never give you indigestion."

WHAT WAS ITS NAME

Two elderly couples were enjoying friendly conversation when one of the men asked the other, "Pete, how was that memory clinic that you went to the other day?"

"It was great," Pete responded. "They taught us about the latest psychological techniques and visualization associations. It was a tremendous help."

"I'm glad to hear that," said George. "What was the clinic called?"

Pete's mind went blank. He could not remember what it was called. Then he said to George, "George what do you call that beautiful fragrant flower with the long stem and thorns?"

"You mean a rose?"

"Yes, that's it!" Pete turned to his wife and said, "Rose, what was the name of that clinic?"

"You're getting old if you can remember when the only bad thing about television was the reception."

CELEBRATES HIS 100th BIRTHDAY

A man was celebrating his 100th birthday, and a local television reporter visited the nursing home to interview him.

"Are you able to get out and walk much?" the reporter asked.

"Well, I certainly walk better today then I could a hundred years ago," he answered with a grin.

HOW OLD IS SHE

A woman's age is hard to tell. It is like the odometer on a car; with hairdos, face-lifts, and the likes, you know that it's been turned back, but you just don't know how far.

FOR YOUR BIRTHDAY

May you have a happy birthday,
May your day be truly blessed,
May you know our dear Lord's presence
And His gift of inward rest.

As you take time to remember
All the way He's led till now,
May your heart be deeply grateful
As in thankfulness you bow.

As you face an unknown future,
Think! He's made you, He will bear;
He will carry and deliver
With omnipotence and care.

With His great and precious promises
May your heart be filled with cheer;
Though there may be times of trouble,
"I will be with you, do not fear!"

So may this another birthday
Draw you closer to our Lord,
As you praise and put your trust in
Your Shield and Exceeding Great Reward.
-- Marjory Windsor

**"Sixty is the age when you begin to realize
how much fun you had when you were thirty."**

"The quickest way to cook your goose is with a boiling temper."

WHEN TO TAKE YOUR MEDICINE

The pharmacist tells an older patron who is paying for her prescription. "Take one of these pills every four hours, or as often as you can get the cap off."

GRANDPA'S PAY MORE

Five year old Billy was visiting his grandparents. Sunday morning, they got their good clothes on and went to church. Being a member of the choir, grandmother took her place with the choir while Billy sat with his grandfather in the congregation.

During the service, grandmother motioned several times to Billy to poke grandfather and keep him awake, but there was no response from him.

After church, Billy's grandmother asked him why he did not do what she had asked, especially since she had given him 50 cents. Billy said, "Grandpa gave me $1.00 to let him sleep."

"A senior adult is one who reaches the age where he has to prove that he is just as good as he never was."

JOB RESUME

* My first job was working in an orange juice factory, but I got canned. I couldn't concentrate.
* Then I worked in the woods as a lumberjack, but I just couldn't hack it, so they gave me the axe.
* After that, I tried to be a tailor, but I just wasn't suited for it, mainly because it was a sew-sew job.
* Next, I tried working in a muffler factory, but that was too exhausting.
* Then, I tried to be a chef. I figured it would add a little spice to my life, but I just didn't have the thyme.
* I attempted to be a deli worker, but any way I sliced it I couldn't cut the mustard.
* My best job was a musician but eventually I found I wasn't noteworthy.
* I studied a long time to become a doctor, but I didn't have any patience.
* Next, was a job in a shoe factory. I tried but I just didn't fit in.
* I became a professional fisherman, but discovered that I couldn't live on my net income.
* I managed to get a good job working for a pool maintenance company, but the work was just too draining.
* So then I got a job in a workout center, but they said I wasn't fit for the job.
* After many years of trying to find steady work, I finally got a job as a historian until I realized there was no future in it.
* My last job was working in Starbucks, but I had to quit because it was always the same old grind.
* So, I tried retirement and found that I'm perfect for the job!!!

"Be glad in the Lord, and rejoice, ye righteous; and shout for joy, all ye that are upright in heart." Psalm 32:11

CELEBRATING 40th ANNIVERSARY

A husband was telling a friend about how he and his wife celebrated their 25th wedding anniversary. "Well, what did you do?" asked his friend.

"Well I took her to Paris to celebrate, said the husband.

"My, that will be hard to beat. What do you plan now for your 40th?"

"Well, I'm going back to Paris to get her!"

"Old age is like a bank account, you withdraw in later life what you have deposited along the way. So my advice to you is to deposit all the happiness you can."

SECRET TO A HAPPY MARRIAGE

A new acquaintance of mine was sharing with me the secret of a happy marriage. "And what is the secret," I asked.

"Well, we go out twice a week to eat in a restaurant. I go on Tuesday and she goes on Thursday!"

DON'T MESS WITH SENIORS

We went to breakfast at a restaurant where the "Seniors' Special" was two eggs, bacon, hash browns and toast for $1.99.

"Sounds good," my wife said. "But I don't want the eggs."

"Then I'll have to charge you two dollars and ninety-nine cents because you're ordering a la carte," the waitress warned her.

"You mean I'd have to pay for not taking the eggs?" my wife asked incredulously. "Then I'll take the special."

"How do you want your eggs?"

"Raw and in the shell!" my wife replied. She took the two eggs home.

"Youth looks ahead, old age looks back, and middle age looks tired."

PATIENCE

A bright, wealthy and relatively healthy old lady of 96 was asked: "Why do you think that God has permitted you to live so long?"

The very wealthy old lady replied, "He is testing the patience of my relatives."

QUESTION AND ANSWER

Grandfather asked his grandson, "Is there anything worse than being old and bent?"

"Yes," replied his grandson, "being young and broke."

FORMULA FOR LIVING

Asked for his formula for long life, Dr. Arthur Judson Brown, Presbyterian minister celebrating his 103rd birthday, quipped, "Don't die."

REFLECTING

It's good to sit, to read, to think
Of years now in the past;
To see the way our God has led
These moments we should grasp.

Reflect upon those early years,
Our home, our school, our play,
Our church, our friends and others
Who have helped us find "The Way."

We've been so blessed, our life so full,
Our hands and hearts we raise
We thank God now for all our years
We sing our songs of praise.

We now rejoice in our today
For health and strength and more
We look in faith to what's ahead
Our Lord we will adore!
- A. Daniel Goldsmith

"Tomorrow's memories come from today's decisions."

POSITIVE OUTLOOK ON LIFE

The 92-year-old, petite, well-poised and proud lady, who is fully dressed each morning by eight o'clock, with her hair fashionably coifed and makeup perfectly applied, even though she is legally blind, moved to a nursing home today. Her husband of 70 years recently passed away, making the move necessary.

After many hours of waiting patiently in the lobby of the nursing home, she smiled sweetly when told her room was ready. As she maneuvered her walker to the elevator, I provided a visual description of her tiny room, including the eyelet sheets that had been hung on her window.

"I love it," she stated with the enthusiasm of an eight-year-old having just been presented with a new puppy.

"Mrs. Jones, you haven't seen the room .... just wait."

"That doesn't have anything to do with it," she replied. "Happiness is something you decide on ahead of time. Whether I like my room or not doesn't depend on how the furniture is arranged. It's how I arrange my mind. I already decided to love it. It's a decision I make every morning when I wake up. I have a choice; I can spend the day in bed recounting the difficulty I have with the parts of my body that no longer work, or get out of bed and be thankful for the ones that do. Each day is a gift, and as long as my eyes open I'll focus on the new day and all the happy memories I've stored away, just for this time in my life."

"A life lived for Christ is the best inheritance we can leave our children."

THREE RULES FOR HAPPINESS

> 1. Free your heart from hatred.
> 2. Free your mind from worries.
> 3. Live simply.

WANT TO GET OLDER

When Konrad Adenauer, chancellor of the Federal Republic of Germany (West Germany), was approaching ninety years of age, he succumbed to a serious cold. He became quite impatient with his personal physician. His doctor said, "I am not a magician, I can't make you young again."

Adenauer retorted, "I haven't asked you to make me younger. All I want is to go on getting older."

"Some people grow old and spread cheer; others just grow old and spread."

A VERY SPECIAL DAY

A couple had been married a good many years. The family was grown and gone. It seemed like the romance had diminished a bit. The husband sat at the breakfast table, and in his usual form was reading the morning newspaper, paying no attention to his wife. Finally, she said, "I bet you don't know what day today is."

He put down his paper, and strongly stated that he certainly did know what today was. He gave her a peck on the cheek and was out the door.

At work he had his secretary order a dozen roses to be sent to his wife. He asked one of the interns to go to the nearest drug store, purchase a five pound box of chocolates and deliver them to his wife.

In the early afternoon he phoned his wife and told her that she did not have to fix dinner as he would be taking her out for their evening meal.

Together they enjoyed a wonderful evening of fine dining. Once at home he devoted his time to his beloved wife and they had a good long chat, talking about the nearly forty years that they had been together, and all of the fun times that they had enjoyed with their family. Eventually they began to retire for the evening. As they were about to bed down for the night, she turned to her husband and said, "Honey, I want to thank you for the most enjoyable 'Ground Hogs Day' that I've ever had."

"An old timer is one who can remember when the village square was a place instead of a person."

TWO QUESTIONS

Last November my phone rang. I said, "Hello." The voice on the other end said, "Are you Anna Jean Smith who attended the old Glenville School in 1945?" I replied, "Yes, sir, I am." Then he said, "Do you remember your grammar school sweetheart who gave you your first kiss?" I said, "Of course I do. A girl never forgets her first kiss." He replied, "Well, you're talking to him."

My heart skipped a beat. He told me he had a photograph of our grade one class and wanted to bring it over the next day. I said, "Wonderful!" I was so excited I didn't sleep a wink.

The next afternoon when I heard a car door slam, I ran to the bathroom to spray on a little more perfume, and with trembling hands I opened the door.

After 65 years, it was love at first sight. We talked for hours and got reacquainted. After several dates he fell on his knees and said, "Honey, I have two questions. First, will you marry me?" I said, "Yes, I'd love to. What's the second question?" He said, "Will you help me up?"

"Most people enjoy living in the past. It is cheaper."

PONDERING OLD AGE

How do I know that my youth is all spent?
Well, my get up and go has got up and went.
But in spite of it all I am able to grin
When I recall where my get up has been.

Old age is golden-so I've heard it said,
But sometimes I wonder when I get into bed,
With my ears in a drawer and my teeth in a cup,
My eyes on the table until I wake up.

Ere sleep dims my eyes I say to myself,
"Is there anything else I should lay on the shelf?"
And I'm happy to say as I close my door,
My friends are the same, perhaps even more.

When I was young, my slippers were red,
I could pick up my heels right over my head.
When I grew older, my slippers were blue,
But still I could dance the whole night through.

But now I am old, my slippers are black,
I walk to the store and puff my way back.
The reason I know my youth is all spent,
My get up and go has got up and went.

But I really don't mind when I think, with a grin,
Of all the grand places my get up has been.
Since I have retired from life's competition,
I accommodate myself with complete repetition.

I get up each morning, and dust off my wits,
Pick up my paper and read the "obits".
If my name is missing, I know I'm not dead,
So I eat a good breakfast and go back to bed

WHICH IS WORSE

Byron's parents, who lived in the path of an oncoming hurricane, sent him to stay with his grandparents for a few days. Two days later the grandparents phoned Byron's parents: "We are returning Byron, send us the hurricane."

OLD AGE IS AROUND THE CORNER

When a man starts making excuses to stay at home instead of going out, old age is just around the corner. In other words, old age is when you don't care where your wife goes, just as long as you don't have to go with her.

"Whether a man winds up with a nest egg or a goose egg depends a lot on the kind of chick he marries."

WHAT WAS IT LIKE

A great grand-niece looked up at her great grand-aunt and sensing her age asked naively, "What did you do when you were alive?"

"When a man's friends begin to compliment him about looking young, he may be sure that they think he is growing old." - Washington Irving

YOU TELL ME I'M GETTING OLD

You tell me I am getting old; I tell you that's not so;
The house I live in is worn out, and that, of course, I know
It's been in use a long, long while, it's weathered many a gale;
I'm really not surprised you think, it's getting somewhat frail.

The color's changing on the roof, the windows getting dim,
The wall's a bit transparent and looking rather thin.
The foundation's not so steady, as once it used to be;
My house is getting shaky, but my house isn't me!

My few short years can't make me old, I feel I'm in my youth;
Eternity lies just ahead, a life of joy and truth.
I'm going to live forever, there, life will go on – it's grand!
You tell me I am getting old? You just don't understand.

The dweller in my little house is young and bright and gay
Just starting on a life to last throughout eternal day.
You only see the outside, which is all that most folks see,
You tell me I am getting old? You've mixed my house with me!
- Dora Johnson

"Age stiffens the joints and thickens some brains."

130

"You're getting old when you're on vacation and your energy runs out before your money does."

THE CLOCK

The clock of life is wound but once,
And no man has the power
To tell just when the hands will stop
At late or early hour.

To lose one's wealth is sad indeed
To lose one's health is more,
To lose one's soul is such a loss
That no man can restore

The present only is our own,
Live, love, toil with a will,
Place no faith in tomorrow, for
The clock may then be still.

FLATTERY

A crusty, ill-tempered old man finally decided to retire at the age of 70. He was given the usual retirement dinner and parting gifts. His associates were joyous at the prospect of his leaving, that they were elaborate with their praise. When the old fellow's time came for him to respond, he stood up and said, "I had no idea that I was held in such high esteem. I have decided to stay on."

"An archaeologist is the best husband a woman can have. The older she gets, the more interested he is in her." - Agatha Christie

LIFE BEGINS AT 80

I have good news for you. "The first 80 years are the hardest. The second 80, as far as my experience goes, is a succession of birthday parties," Frank Lauback. "Everybody wants to carry your luggage and help you up the steps. If you forget anyone's name, or forget to fill an appointment, or promise to be at two or three places at the same time, or spell words wrongly, you can explain, you are 80! If you spill soup on your necktie or fail to shave one side of your face, or if your shoes do not match, or you take the other man's hat by mistake, or carry a letter around for a week before mailing it, YOU ARE 80! It is a great deal better than being 65 or 70. At that time they expect you to move to a little house in Florida and become a discontented, grumbling 'has been'. But if you survive till 80, everybody is surprised that you can talk above a whisper. At 70 people get mad at you for every mistake. At 80 they forgive everything."

131

"Aspire to inspire before you expire."

CONTRAST BETWEEN BYRON AND PAUL

Lord Byron wrote before he died: "My days in the yellow leaf, the fruit, the flower of life, is gone, the worm, the canker and the grief are mine alone."

The apostle Paul wrote before he died: "I have fought a good fight, I have finished my course, I have kept the faith; henceforth there is laid up for me a crown of righteousness." C. Perren

A REAL BARGAIN

My wife Carol and I were visiting her 95 year old grandfather, when he asked us to take him to the mall, to buy a new hat. Carol took me aside. "I'm worried that he doesn't have enough money, and he'll be very embarrassed," she said. So I asked the salesperson to tell my wife's grandfather that whichever hat he chose cost $15.00. I would pay the difference.

Grandpa picked out a $60.00 hat and was charged $15.00. After he left, I paid the other $45.00. Later he said, "What a bargain! The last one that I bought there cost me $60.00.

"One of the greatest pleasures of growing old is the freedom we enjoy from life insurance salesmen."

SURGICAL TOOLS

To address an emergency call, a doctor came to see a rich elderly patient at his home, who was screaming with extreme stomach pain and was surrounded by many anxious relatives. The Doctor kicked all the relatives out of the room and closed the door. He alone was with the patient.

After a while he came out and asked, "Please give me a pair of scissors." People gave him stainless steel scissors. He again went inside, closed the door and soon came back. He said, "Please give me a hammer." He got one. A number of times he repeated the routine of going inside, closing the door and then coming back again for a new tool.

Finally he came outside one more time and asked, "Please give me a screw driver."

The oldest son could not stand it any more and lost his patience. In a crying voice he pleaded, "Doctor please tell us what has happened to our dear father. Will he live? Could we open his will?"

The doctor said, "I don't know that yet. I am still trying to open my stupid bag - I lost the key."

"Elderberries have more fun than younger berries."

"We must learn from the past, but we must not live in the past."

MARRIAGE COUNSELING

We were celebrating Grandpa and Grandma's 50th wedding anniversary. The topic got around to what kind of counseling they had. Grandma said, "We never had any counseling. We didn't need it and we've had a great relationship. You see Grandpa was a communications major in college and I majored in theatre arts. He communicates real well and I just act like I'm listening."

A MARRIAGE SECRET

A couple had been married for 45 years and had raised a brood of 11 children and were blessed with 22 grandchildren. When asked the secret for staying together all that time, the wife replied, "Many years ago we made a promise to each other: the first one to pack up and leave had to take all the kids."

"Grandma and Grandpa met in a revolving door and started going around together."

HAPPY BIRTHDAY ELSIE

I play Scrabble regularly with seven other women, most of whom are 70 or older. Recently we celebrated the birthday of our oldest member by taking her out to lunch. When the waitress came to take our order, one of the women said to her, "This is a very special occasion. It's Elsie's ninety-second birthday."

The waitress made seven instant enemies and one fast friend by asking the question, "Which one of you is Elsie?"

THANKFUL OR UNTHANKFUL

There are four kinds of seniors. There are the kind that are forever grumbling and complaining. Have you met this kind? They are the kind that brighten up a room just by leaving it. Then there are those who live lives of ingratitude. They do not complain, but they never give thanks to God for His many blessings. That's a little better than the grumblers. Then there are the seniors that thank God when something good happens. That's a better level. However, the highest level is those who are grateful for all things at all times. That is the secret of a happy and productive life. What level do you belong to?

"It does not pay to get sour as you get old. I pity a man who lives in the past. He lives on stale manna. He gets stunted." - Evangelist D. L. Moody

BANK ARRANGEMENTS

Dear Sir:

I am writing to thank you for bouncing my check with which I endeavored to pay my plumber. By my calculations, three "nanoseconds" must have elapsed between his presenting his check and the automatic deposit of my monthly pension. You are to be commended for seizing that brief window of opportunity, and also for debiting my account $30 by way of penalty for the inconvenience caused to your bank.

My thankfulness springs from the manner in which this incident has caused me to rethink my errant financial ways. I noticed that whereas I personally attend to your telephone calls and letters, when I try to contact you, I am confronted by the impersonal, overcharging, pre-recorded, faceless entity which your bank has become.

From now on, I, like you, choose only to deal with a flesh-and-blood person. My mortgage and loan payments will no longer be automatic, but will arrive at your bank by check, addressed personally and confidentially to an employee at your bank whom you must nominate. Under the Postal Act it will be an offence for any other person to open such an envelope. Please find attached an Application Contact Status which I require your chosen employee to complete.

I am sorry it runs to eight pages, but in order that I know as much about him or her as your bank knows about me, there is no alternative. All copies of his/her medical history must be countersigned by a Notary Public, and the mandatory details of his/her financial situation (income, debts, assets, and liabilities) must be accompanied by documented proof. In due course, I will issue your employee with a PIN number which he/she must quote in dealings with me. I regret that it cannot be shorter than 28 digits but, again, I have modeled it on the number of button presses required of me to access my account balance on your phone bank service. As they say, imitation is the sincerest form of flattery.

Let me level the playing field even further. When you call me, press buttons as follows: (1) To make an appointment to see me. (2) To query a missing payment. (3) To transfer the call to my living room in case I am there. (4) To transfer the call to my bedroom in case I am sleeping. (5) To transfer the call to my toilet in case I am attending to nature. (6) To transfer the call to my mobile phone if I am not at home. (7) To leave a message on my computer. (A password to access my computer is required. A password will be communicated to you at a later date to the Authorized Contact.) (8) To return to the main menu and to listen to options 1 through 7. (9) To make a general complaint or inquiry, the contact will then be put on hold, pending the attention of my automated answering service.

Uplifting music will play, if you need to wait on the line. Regrettably, but again following your example, I must also levy an establishment fee to cover the setting up of this new arrangement. Your Humble Client.   - A Senior Citizen

"Age is like love, it cannot be hidden."

DO YOU NEED A PEN

A patient at the dental office where I was a receptionist stopped by my desk to pay her bill. She began rummaging through her purse, as so many patients do when they have a check to write.

"Do you need a pen?" I asked, offering her the use of mine.

"Yes, thank you," she replied. She took it, put it in her handbag and proceeded to pay in cash

"Goodbye tension, hello pension."

WEDDING ANNIVERSARY GIFT

A couple, celebrating their 50th wedding anniversary, was given a toaster oven. They had never had a toaster oven before. The first day after their big anniversary the husband tried it out. Almost immediately, smoke billowed out of the toaster. "Get the owner's manual!" he shouted.

"I can't find it anywhere!" she cried, searching through the box.

"Oops!" came a voice from the kitchen. "Well, the toast is fine, but the owner's manual is burnt to a crisp."

DENTURES DON'T HURT

A couple of old guys were golfing when one said he was going to Dr. Taylor for a new set of dentures in the morning. His friend remarked that he had gone to the same dentist a few years before.

"Is that so?" the first said. "Did he do a good job?"

"Well, I was on the course yesterday when the fellow on the ninth hole hooked a shot," he said. "The ball must have been going 200 mph when it hit me in the stomach. That," he added, "was the first time in two years my teeth didn't hurt."

DIDN'T KNOW HOW GOOD IT WAS

Methusaleh didn't know how good he had it. He lived 969 years and never had to fill one single income tax form.

"We have always needed old people to keep things from going too fast and young people to keep them from going too slow. Youth has fire and age has light and we need them both." - Dr. Vance Havner

HELP APPRECIATED

A man writing at the post office desk was approached by an older fellow with a post card in his hand. The old man said, "Sir, I'm sorry to bother you but could you address this post card for me? My arthritis is acting up today and I can't even hold a pen."

"Certainly sir," said the younger man, "I'd be glad to."

He wrote out the address and also agreed to write a short message and sign the card for the man. Finally, the younger man asked, "Now, is there anything else I can do for you?"

The old fellow thought about it for a moment and said, "Yes, at the end could you just add, 'PS: Please excuse the sloppy hand-writing.'?"

GRANDPA AND TELE-MARKETERS

The telephone marketer selling basement waterproofing must have thought she'd died and gone to heaven when she reached my very polite and patient grandfather. At the end of her long sales pitch, she asked, grandpa, "Do you mind if we send out someone to give you an estimate?"

"Not at all," grandpa said.

"When would be a good time?" she asked.

Grandpa answered, "Just as soon as I dig a basement."

40th ANNIVERSARY CLASS REUNION

Joe, Sam, and Bill had travelled together to attend their high school graduation's 50th anniversary. They were sharing a large suite at the top of a 30 story hotel.

After a long day of travelling they booked into their room and then went out for dinner. After their meal, and arriving back at their hotel, they were shocked to learn that the elevators in their hotel were broken and they would have to climb 30 flights of stairs to get to their room.

Joe said to Sam and Bill, "Let's break the monotony of this unpleasant task by concentrating on something interesting. I'll tell jokes for 10 floors, Sam can sing songs for the next 10 floors, and Bill can tell sad stories for the rest of the way."

At the 11th floor, Joe stopped telling jokes and Sam began to sing. At the 21st floor, Sam stopped singing and it was Bill's turn to tell sad stories.

"I will tell my saddest story first," Bill said. "I left our room key in the car!"

"As soon as you feel too old to do a thing, go out and do it. As soon as you feel critical, say something kind in a kindly way. As soon as you feel neglected, send a cheery note to a friend." - Oliver Wilson

THE CHURCH – MY WAY

Bill likes a sermon short and sweet,
Mary wants it only once a week.
Sue prefers one an hour long,
Karl says "preach it loud and strong."

Jane wants music with lots of beat
George likes it better if we stomp our feet,
Marge prefers soft melodic tunes
Pete, majestic anthems to fill the room.

Pat worships best in a church that's small,
Abe's attitude is come one come all.
Lynn wants programs for everyone,
Joe is sold on a one on one.

When it comes to money that's another thing
Ken, Lil, and Curt would give everything
While some of the others would keep all they can,
And fail to fulfill God's wonderful plan.

Is it any wonder that we don't agree
And you don't like what pleases me?
Why not quit? Don't pray or pay
Until you're sure to have your way.

But oh how foolish that would be
To have a church for only me;
Christ came to seek and save the lost
We must work and pray at any cost.

When God is seated in His rightful place
We all can serve, He gives the grace,
Even in times, when hard to swallow
The Church is God's, let's seek to follow.
                    - A. Daniel Goldsmith

"God's house is a hive for workers, not a nest for drones."

"The prime of life is that fleeting time between green and overripe."

FIX THE FAX

An older gentleman bought a FAX machine and felt that it needed some repair. He asked his neighbor if he knew anything about FAX machines. The neighbor said that he knew a little bit and inquired as to what the problem was.

"Well," said the older gent, "I sent a fax, and the recipient called back to say that all that she received was a cover-sheet and a blank page. I tried it again, and the same thing happened."

"How did you load the sheet?" the neighbor asked.

"Well it is a pretty sensitive memo, and I didn't want anyone else to read it by accident, so I folded it so only the recipient would have to open it and read it."

"A gossiper is a person with a sense of rumor."

A FEW BENEFITS OF OLD AGE

In a hostage situation you are likely to be released first.
People call at 9 p.m. and ask, "Did I wake you?"
There's nothing left to learn the hard way.
Things you buy now won't wear out.
You can eat dinner at 4:00pm.
You can't remember the last time you laid on the floor to watch television.
You consider coffee one of the most important things in life.
You can constantly talk about the price of gasoline.
You enjoy hearing about other people's operations.
You got cable for the weather channel.
You have a party and the neighbors don't even realize it.
You no longer think of speed limits as a challenge.
You give lots of money to charities.
You have an age advantage whenever you need it.
You are not expected to keep up with technology or understand it.
You get travel and entertainment discounts.
Your investment in health insurance is finally beginning to pay off.
People come to you for help with their antique cars.

HOW WOULD YOU LIKE TO BE REMEMBERED

Dr. Billy Graham, the evangelist, was asked on his 75th birthday how he would like to be remembered. He responded by saying, "Someone who was fun to be around."

"You've reached middle age when all you exercise is caution."

WHAT HAPPENED

"What happened?" asked the hospital visitor to his elderly neighbor, who was heavily bandaged and sitting up in bed.

"Well, I went down to Margate with a couple of my grandsons on the weekend and decided to take a ride on the roller coaster. As we came up to the top of the highest loop, I noticed a little sign by the side of the track. I tried to read it but it was very small and I couldn't make it out. I was so curious that I decided to go around again, but we went by so quickly that I couldn't see what the sign said. By now, I was determined to read that sign so I went around a third time. As we reached the top, I stood up in the car to get a better view."

"And did you manage to see what the sign said this time?" asked the visitor.

"Yes."

"What did it say?"

It said, "Don't stand up in the car!"

"Old friends are good therapy." - A. Daniel Goldsmith

MY ANSWER

In the summer of 1964 I had the privilege of meeting and hearing the famous Dr. Walter L. Wilson. He was the guest speaker at the Biola Family Week at The Firs Bible Conference Center in Bellingham, WA. Dr. Wilson was one of America's best-loved Bible teachers who was profound in his simplicity. He used homey illustrations and had a unique sense of humor.

One day when I greeted him, I asked that age old question, "How are you?" Dr. Wilson handed me a slip of paper on which was printed "My Answer." This is what he had printed under the heading "My Answer."

"You ask me, 'How are you?' and I reply at once and with pleasure: My appendix is in and my tonsils are out. My epiglottis is working nicely. My sinuses are clear and my joints all fully lubricated. My digestion is fine and my lachrymal glands are working. My spleen is O.K. and my pancreas is in good condition. My feet are free from corns and bunions and my heart is beating with regular rhythm. My breathing is also regular. My soul is saved by Jesus Christ and I am His property. Now if you wish further information let me know, and also let me know what you will do with this information. Walter L. Wilson, M.D." - A. Daniel Goldsmith

"All some people do is grow old."

BIBLE TRANSLATORS

A seminary student went to visit his grandmother. Thinking that he would have a little fun with her he said, "Grandma, you know that the Bible was written in Hebrew and Greek and translated by scholars into English. How do you know that it was translated correctly?"

"Oh, Jamie," she said, "don't worry. I've translated quite a few verses myself."

"Life is like a hot bath, the longer you stay in it the more wrinkles you get."

A SMART DOCTOR

A new doctor had arrived in town and claimed that he could cure anything and everyone. Everyone was happy with this doctor, except Mr. Thompson the skeptic.

So grumpy old Mr. Thompson went to visit this 'miracle doctor' to prove that he wasn't anybody special. When it was time for his appointment he told the doctor, "Hey, doc, I've lost my sense of taste. I can't taste nothin', so what are ya goin' to do?"

The doctor scratched his head and mumbled to himself a little, then told Mr. Thompson, "What you need is jar number 47."

So the doctor brought the jar out, opened it, and told Mr. Thompson to taste it. He tasted it and immediately spit it out, "This is gross!" he yelled. "Looks like I just restored your sense of taste Mr. Thompson," said the doctor. So Mr. Thompson went home.... very mad.

One month later, Mr. Thompson decided to go back to the doctor and try once again to expose him as a fake, by complaining of a new problem. "Doc," he started, "I can't remember anything!" Thinking he had the doctor stumped now, he waited as the doctor scratched his head, mumbled to himself a little, and told Mr. Thompson, "What you need is jar number 47, it's......"

But before the doctor could finish his sentence, Mr. Thompson was cured and fled the room!

SENIORS ARE VALUABLE

We have silver in our hair.
We have gold in our teeth.
We have stones in our kidneys.
We have lead in our feet.
And we are loaded with natural gas.

"A warm smile and wholesome laughter have great face value."

BUS TRANSFER

The elderly woman handed the bus driver her transfer. "This isn't any good. It's dated yesterday," said the bus driver.

"Oh, I didn't know that you were that late!" snapped the woman.

"Three signs of old age: First, loss of memory, and... I forget the other two."

ASSETS

My husband refused to learn how to operate a computer. I tried to get him to realize how important it is, since all our financial records are stored on disks.

"What if something happens to me?" I asked him. "You wouldn't know what our assets are."

"Honey," he replied, "if something happened to you, I wouldn't need any money."

"Middle age is when your age starts to show around your middle." - Bob Hope

APPLAUSE

My grandfather, who was a famous football coach, together with grandma were on vacation in the State of Maine. When they walked into a movie theatre and sat down, the handful of people there applauded. He thought to himself, "I can't believe it. People recognize me all the way up here."

Then a man came over to him and said, "Thanks for coming. They won't start the movie unless we have ten paying people or more."

SPEED OF TIME

When as a child I slept and wept, Time crept;
When as a youth I laughed and talked, Time walked;
When I became a full grown man, Time ran;
And older as I daily grew, Time flew;
Soon I shall find in traveling on, Time gone.
- From an English sundial

"The advantage of a bad memory is that one enjoys several times the same things for the first time."

MISUNDERSTOOD

Grandpa stepped up behind grandma and said, "Would you like to go out girl?"

Not even turning around grandma said, "Oh, yes, I'd love to!"

They had a wonderful evening and it wasn't until the end of it that grandpa confessed that his question was directed to the family dog.

"Experience is what you've got when you're too old to get a job."

RETIRED PASTOR PREACHING

A retired pastor was asked to fill in for a pastor who was on vacation. Having lost all track of time, he droned on and on. He had covered most of Hebrews chapter eleven, verse by verse and was now at verse 32. When he read the words of that verse, *"And what more shall I say?"*

Someone in the back pew said, say "Amen."

SNOW REMOVAL

One winter morning during breakfast a retired couple living in Minnesota was listening to the radio. They heard the announcer say, "We are going to have 8 to 10 inches of snow today. You must park your car on the even-numbered side of the street, so the snowplows can get through." So the wife went out and moved her car.

A week later while they are eating breakfast again, the radio announcer said, "We are expecting 10 to 12 inches of snow today. You must park your car on the odd-numbered side of the street, so the snowplows can get through." The wife went out and moved her car again.

The next week they are again having breakfast, when the radio announcer says, "We are expecting 12 to 14 inches of snow today. You must park..." Then the electric power went off. The wife was very upset, and with a worried look on her face she said, "Honey, I don't know what to do. Which side of the street do I need to park on so the snowplows can get through?"

With the love and understanding in his voice, the husband replied, "Why don't you just leave the car in the garage this time?"

GOOD EXCUSE FOR SPEEDING

Did you hear about the 83 year old woman who talked herself out of a speeding ticket by telling the young officer that she had exceeded the speed limit because she had to get there before she forgot where she was going?

THE CRAZIEST LANGUAGE

We begin with box and the plural is boxes;
But the plural of ox should be oxen not oxes.
Then one fowl is a goose, but two are called geese,
Yet the plural of moose should never be meese.

You may find a lone mouse or a nest full of mice,
Yet the plural of house is houses, not hice.
If the plural of man is always called men
Why shouldn't the plural of pan be called pen?

If I spoke of my foot and show you my feet,
And I give you a boot, would a pair be called beet?
If one is a tooth and a whole set are teeth
Why shouldn't the plural of booth be called beeth?

That one may be that, and three would be those,
Yet hat in the plural would never be hose.
We speak of a brother and also of brethren,
But though we say mother, we never say methren.

Then the masculine pronouns are he, his and him,
But imagine the feminine, she, shis and shim.
So English, I fancy that you will agree,
Is the craziest language you ever did see.

"A day without laughter is a day wasted."

RETIRED BOOMERS

A retired "boomer" was hit hard by the recent economic down turn and decided that he needed to supplement his meager pension. He learned, through some friends, that the ape in the local zoo had died. The ape was a big attraction and since the zoo officials were unable to secure another ape immediately, they were looking for someone who would wear an ape costume and perform in the cage. The young retiree thought he was energetic enough to do so, and furthermore the pay was very attractive.

With a brief training period, he was soon in the cage and doing well with his stunts. None of the spectators were any the wiser. He looked like an ape, acted like an ape and satisfied the zoo officials. After about two weeks on the job, he was swinging back and forth and each day seemed to swing higher than the day before. One day he overdid it. He reached a new height, lost control of his grip on the swing and landed in the lion's cage next door. When the lion started strutting towards the fallen ape, the man in the ape suit began to scream and holler for help. Whereupon, the lion said "Shut up, or we'll both lose our jobs."

ARE YOU STILL ALIVE

A reporter asked my 90 year old daddy, who lived in Casper, Wyoming, "Mr. Simpson, have you lived all your life in Casper?" My father testily replied, "Not yet!" So if you wonder whether you still have a mission in life, just ask yourself one question. Are you still alive?
- Senator Alan Simpson

"What most torments me about the foolishness of my youth, is not the crazy things I've done, but the fact that I can't go back and do them again."

HE HAD AN EXCUSE

A couple had been married for many years. They lived in the same house all those years. It was their custom to take an evening walk every day in an open field behind their house. One evening, they came to a little creek that ran across the open field. "Do you remember how I used to jump that creek flatfooted?"

"Yes," replied the wife, "but that was when we were younger."

"I can still do it," he exclaimed.

Before she could stop him, he took his stance on one side of the creek, squatted down, and leaped forward. Both feet landed squarely in the middle of the creek. As he waded out of the muddy creek and started back to the house, he commented to his wife, "That's strange! I guess I just didn't notice that the creek was getting wider through the years."

COMPLIMENTS THE MINISTER

A minister was talking to an older lady who worked hard as a cleaning lady. He told her how glad he was to see her in her place in church every Sunday morning. She was so attentive to his sermons. "Yes," she replied, "it is such a rest after a hard week's work to come to church, sit on the soft cushions and not think about anything."

"Experience is what causes older people to make new mistakes instead of the old ones."

GRANDCHILDREN GO FOR CAR RIDE

My wife and I decided to take the grand-children for a car ride. The two grand-children were bickering in the backseat. Our five year old grand-daughter was in a particularly bossy mood, telling her seven year old brother where to put his toys, where to sit, and how to buckle his seat belt. After putting up with her orders, he finally said, "Who do you think you are? My wife?"

"Christians are not citizens of earth trying to get to heaven, but citizens of heaven making their way through this world. "
- Dr. Vance Havner

PROBLEM WITH THE SPEAKER

A guest speaker was speaking in church one Sunday and while he was speaking there was a lot of feedback and crackling sound with his microphone. He was trying to get rid of it when someone came up to him from the sound booth with a note. The note said, "We have found the problem. There is a screw loose in the speaker!"

"Nothing weakens the truth more than stretching it."

REMOTE CONTROL

"Cash, check or charge?" I asked, after folding items the woman wished to purchase. As she fumbled for her wallet, I noticed a remote control for a television set in her purse. "So, do you always carry your TV remote with you?" I asked.

"No," she replied, "but my husband is retired and he refuses to go shopping with me. I figured this was the worst thing I could do to him legally."

"Good better best, let me never rest, until my good is better and my better is best."

RETIREE RECEIVES GOLD WATCH

As the president of the company presented the retiree with his gold watch, he said: "As a symbol of our gratitude, we have created this special gold watch just for you. It will serve as a reminder of your many years with this company. It needs a lot of winding up. It is always a little late, and every day at a quarter to five, it stops working."

ROOF LEAKED

Old Mr. Gable had a leak in the roof over his dining room, so he called a repairman to take a look at it. "When did you first notice the leak?" the repairman inquired.

Mr. Gable scowled, "Last night, when it took me two hours to finish my soup!"

"It's never too late to have a happy childhood. But the second one is up to you and no one else." - Regina Brett

145

NEGATIVE ATTITUDE

A hair stylist, with a very negative view of everything, was giving a perm to a recently retired woman who was preparing for her first overseas trip. "What airline are you taking? she asked.

"I am flying on Greater Europe Airlines," said the woman.

"Greater Europe Airlines," exclaimed the stylist, "I would never ever fly with Greater Europe again. Their service is the poorest of the poor. Where are you headed?"

"Among many places in Europe, I am really excited about going to Rome," she responded.

"Never again would I go to Rome. The streets are dirty, the people are so rude," said the hair dresser. "What hotel are you planning on staying at?"

"I'm booked at the Dominique Courtyard."

"The Dominique Courtyard! That's the last place in the world that you should sleep. The service is very poor and the rooms are not the cleanest. The last time that I was there the elevator was not working. If I ever did go to Rome again, I would definitely not stay there. By the way, do you plan on seeing the Pope?" she asked.

"Yes, I do."

"Well, I'll tell you that is the one good thing about Rome. We found a back door where the Pope can be seen when he is going out to make a speech to the many folks gathered. If you take that door, you might even get to talk with him." Well, the retiree went to Europe, toured England, France, Germany, Italy and the Vatican. When she returned back to her home, she went to her hair stylist to get a hair set.

"Well, how was your trip?" her stylist asked.

"Everything was far better than I had ever imagined, the flight, hotels and I loved Rome."

"Did you get to see the Pope?"

"Yes, I did what you said. I went to that back door and he was only about two feet away."

"What did he say to you?"

"There were several others there so he only asked me one question."

"What did he ask you?"

"He said, who on earth gave you that hair perm?"

GRANDMA'S SHOES

When I was very little, all the grandmas that I knew
All walked around this world in ugly grandma shoes.
You know the ones I speak of, those black clunky heeled king,
They just looked so very awful that it weighed upon my mind.

For I knew, when I grew old, I'd have to wear those shoes,
I'd think of that, from time to time it seemed like such bad news.
I never was a rebel I wore saddle shoes to school,
And next came ballerinas then the sandals, pretty cool.

And then came spikes with pointed toes then platforms, very tall,
As each new fashion came along I wore them, one and all.
But always, in the distance, looming in my future, there
Was that awful pair of ugly shoes, the kind that grandmas wear.

I eventually got married and then I became a Mom
Our kids grew up and left, and when their children came along,
I knew I was a grandma and the time was drawing near
When those clunky, black, old lace up shoes was what I'd have to wear.

How could I do my gardening, or take my morning hike?
I couldn't even think about: How would I ride my bike?
But fashions kept evolving and one day I realized
That the shape of things to come was changing, right before my eyes.

And now when I go shopping what I see, fills me with glee
For in my jeans and Reeboks I'm as comfy as can be.
And I look at all these teenage girls and there, upon their feet
Are clunky, black, old grandma shoes and they really think they're neat.

"Life isn't tied with a bow, but it's still a gift." - Regina Brett

LOST IN NOVA SCOTIA

Two American tourists were driving through Nova Scotia. As they were approaching Shubenacadie (shoe-been-aack-id-dee), they started arguing about the pronunciation of the town's name. They argued back and forth until they stopped for lunch. As they stood at the counter, one tourist asked the employee, ""Before we order, could you please settle an argument for us? Would you please pronounce where we are... ver-r-ry slo-o-owly?"

The waitress leaned over the counter and said: "Tiiimmmmm Hoorrrrttoooonnns..."

ONE GOOD EXCUSE

A senior citizen drove his brand new Corvette convertible out of the dealership and past the Tim Horton's donut shop.

Taking off down the Trans Canada Highway, he floored it to 120 kph, enjoying the wind blowing through what little hair he had left.

"Amazing!" he thought as he flew down the highway, pushing the pedal to the metal even more. Looking in his rear view mirror, he saw a Royal Canadian Mounted Police behind him, with red and blue lights flashing and siren blaring.

"I can get away from him, no problem!" thought the elderly nut case as he floored it to 130 kph, then 140, then 150 kph. Suddenly, he thought, "What on earth am I doing? I'm too old for this nonsense!" He pulled over to the side of the road and waited for the RCMP officer to catch up with him.

Pulling in behind him, the officer walked up to the driver's side of the Corvette, looked at his watch and said, "Sir, my shift ends in 30 minutes. Today is Friday. If you can give me a reason why you were speeding that I've never heard before, I'll let you go."

The man, looking very seriously at the Mountie, said, "A couple of years ago, my wife ran off with an RCMP officer. I thought you were bringing her back."

"Have a good day, Sir," said the Mountie.

"Old age arrives suddenly, as does the snow. One morning, on awakening, one realizes that everything is white."

THE PREACHER SAID NOTHING

After the visiting preacher finished, a woman came up and said, "You were much better than the preacher we had last Sunday. He spoke for an hour and said nothing."

"Thank you," the visiting preacher replied.

"Yes," she continued. "You did it in fifteen minutes."

LAUGH AT ACCENT

One of the top designers in the California Division of Highways was a Russian emigrant whose English was imperfect. He once addressed his fellow designers at a seminar saying: "I have not usual joke to start, so I geeve permission you laugh at my accent."

"Dieters are people who get up in the morning and the first thing they say is 'mirror, mirror on the dresser, do I look a little lesser?"

MIRACLE CURE

Doctor Bloom, who was known for miraculous cures for arthritis, had a waiting room full of people when a little old lady, completely bent over in half, shuffled in slowly, leaning on her cane. When her turn came, she went into the doctor's office, and, amazingly, emerged within half an hour walking completely erect with her head held high.

A woman in the waiting room, who had seen all this, walked up to the little old lady and said, "It's a miracle! You walked in bent in half and now you're walking erect. What did that doctor do?"

She answered, "Miracle? He gave me a longer cane."

LOOKING BACK

A father, as he looked back on his life once said: "If I had it to do all over again, I'd love my wife more in front of my children. I'd laugh with my children more. I'd listen more, even to the youngest child. I'd be more honest about my own weaknesses and stop pretending perfection. I would pray differently for my children. I would be more encouraging and bestow more praise. And finally, if I had it to do all over again, I would use every ordinary thing that happened in every ordinary day to point my children to God." We may still have time to change.

"It's good to have things that money can buy, provided we don't lose the things that money can't buy." - Dr. Warren W. Wiersbe

WERE THE GOOD OLD DAYS REALLY THE GOOD SLOW WAYS

Life has become so hectic, it keeps us on the run!
What is it that we really gain when all is said and done?
Why can't we have some good new days enjoy the here and now,
Just realize that every day has something to bestow?

So day by day, be joyful make every day worth while
You'll be a help to others if you meet them with a smile
These days will then become the memories we hold dear
And great will be our store of joys as we go from year to year. [5]
-Nina Wakelin

"It would be a good thing if young people were wise and old people were strong, but God has arranged things better." - Martin Luther

I HAD A MOM LIKE THAT

Mom and Dad were watching TV when Mom said, "I'm tired, and its' getting late. I think I'll go to bed."

She went to the kitchen to make sandwiches for the next day's lunches, rinsed out the popcorn bowls, took meat out of the freezer for supper the following evening, checked the cereal box levels, filled the sugar container, put spoons and bowls on the table and started the coffee pot for brewing the next morning.

She then put some wet clothes into the dryer, put a load of clothes in the wash, ironed a shirt and secured a loose button. She picked up the newspapers strewn on the floor, picked up the game pieces left on the table and put the telephone book back into the drawer. She watered the plants, emptied a wastebasket and hung up a towel to dry.

She yawned and stretched and headed for the bedroom. She stopped by the desk and wrote a note to the teacher, counted out some cash for the field trip, and pulled a textbook out from hiding under the chair. She signed a birthday card for a friend, addressed and stamped the envelope and wrote a quick note for the grocery store. She put both near her purse.

Mom then washed her face, put on moisturizer, brushed and flossed her teeth and trimmed her nails. Hubby called, "I thought you were going to bed."

"I'm on my way," she said. She put some water into the dog's dish and put the cat outside, then made sure the doors were locked. She looked in on each of the kids and turned out a bedside lamp, hung up a shirt, threw dome dirty socks in the hamper, and had a brief conversation with the one child still doing homework.

In the bed room, she set the alarm, laid out clothing for the next day, straightened up the shoe rack. She added three things to her list of things to do for tomorrow.

About that time, hubby turned off the TV and announced to no one in particular "I'm going to bed," and he did.

"Grandpa's in the take out business. He takes out the garbage."

GET BETTER

A retired man who volunteers to entertain patients in nursing homes and hospitals went to Maimonides Hospital in Brooklyn and took his portable keyboard along. He told some jokes and sang some funny songs for the patients. When he finished and was saying his good-byes, he said, "I hope you get better."

One elderly gentleman replied, "I hope you get better, too."

**"At this stage of life you can still pick your friends,
but don't pick them to pieces."**

THE OLD FARMER WAS FINE

An old farmer was in court trying to get damages from an accident in which he had been hurt. Someone had crossed the median and hit his pick up truck. He was in court and was being cross examined by an attorney. The attorney said, "I want to ask you a question. Is it or is it not true that immediately after the accident you told the police that you were fine?"

"I want to tell you that I was on my way to market. I had my cow Billy in the back of the pick up."

The attorney said, "Look, I don't want to know everything, I just want you to answer my question. Is it or is it not true that immediately after the accident you told the officers that you were fine?"

"Well, said the farmer, I was on my way to market. I had my cow Billy in the back of the pick up.."

"Your honor," said the attorney, "would you please instruct this man to respond to my question?"

"Well," said the judge, "I think that I'm going to let him tell his story. Just go ahead, sir."

"As I was saying, I was on my way to market and this car crossed the median and hit me and I flew out one way and my cow flew out the other way. I was lying there barely conscious. I heard the sirens and then I heard the police officers talking as they were looking at my cow. One of them said, 'I think that this cow is damaged beyond repair and is in terrible misery. He took out his revolver and shot the cow. Then they came over to me and asked me how I was doing. I said, 'I WAS FINE'!"

GRANDPA'S DRIVING RECORD

Grandpa had an exceptionally good driving record. He had only ever received one speeding ticket in his entire 62 years of driving. One day he was driving through a main intersection and passed a traffic camera and saw it flash.

Astounded that he had been caught speeding when he was doing the speed limit, he went around the block and going even slower, he again passed by the camera. The camera flashed. He couldn't believe it. So once more he went around the block and this time around he drove a snail's pace as he passed the camera. Again he saw the camera flash. He assumed that it was malfunctioning and so drove on home.

Four weeks later he received three traffic fines in the mail, all for not wearing a seatbelt.

"Men have three basic hairstyles: parted, unparted, and departed."

HE HAD TO BEHAVE

My uncle Al told me about a fellow in a coffee shop in Saskatoon, Saskatchewan who proudly announced that he had recently been the center of attention when he celebrated his 92nd birthday. Uncle Al, who was present, topped that conversation by telling those drinking their coffee that his brother Nick, who still lives on his own, had just celebrated his 93rd birthday. Pausing for emphasis, Uncle Al added, "but Nick had to behave at his party, because his mother was present." Pearl Lutzko, Nick and Al's mother is officially the oldest living person in the province of Saskatchewan. She was 111 years old February 15th, 2010. [6] - Brenda DiRezze

"Old age is something everybody else reaches before you do."

SOMETHING WONDERFUL

Old age occurs the moment you realize there isn't something wonderful about to happen around the corner. In some people this occurs very soon, in others, not at all.

"We grow old not so much by living, but by losing interest in living."

SING SING PRISON

A socialite was having a book written about her family's history. Much to her horror she discovered that one of her grandfathers had been electrocuted in Sing Sing prison. She was very ashamed of this bit of history and did her best to hide the truth. So the following statement appeared in her book: "One of my grandfathers occupied a chair of applied electricity in one of America's best known institutions. He was very much attached to his position and literally died in the harness."

CHILD NEEDED SOME FRESH AIR

I read of a 54-year-old grandma in the Florida Keys who was spotted driving around the parking lot with her three-year-old grand-daughter perched atop her Lexus. According to the deputies who arrested her, Brenda Bouschet said she "was just giving the child some air and letting her have fun." The child was in no danger, of course, as Brenda had one hand out the window, holding onto a leg. [7] - Phil Callaway

DYING WITH LAUGHTER

A retired surgeon said to me on a plane, "I've practiced medicine for fifty-eight years and I've never known a person to die from laughter." - Roy B. Zuck

"Older people know more about being young than young people know about being old." - Dr. Mark Lee

LANGUAGE FROM THE 50's AND 60's

"Fender skirts!" When I was a kid, I considered it such a funny term. Made me think of a car in a dress. Thinking about fender skirts started me thinking about other words that quietly disappear from our language with hardly a notice, like "curb feelers" and "steering knobs."

Remember "Continental kits?" They were rear bumper extenders and spare tire covers that were supposed to make any car as cool as a Lincoln Continental.

When did we quit calling them "emergency brakes?" At some point "parking brake" became the proper term. But I miss the hint of drama that went with "emergency brake."

I'm sad, too, that almost all the old folks are gone who would call the accelerator the "foot feed."

Here's a phrase I heard all the time in my youth but never anymore –"store-bought." Of course, just about everything is store-bought these days. But once it was bragging material to have a store-bought dress or a store-bought bag of candy.

"Coast to coast" is a phrase that once held all sorts of excitement and now means almost nothing. Now we take the term "worldwide" for granted. This floors me.

On a smaller scale, "wall-to-wall" was once a magical term in our homes. In the '50s, everyone covered their hardwood floors with, wow, wall-to-wall carpeting! Today, everyone replaces their wall-to-wall carpeting with hardwood floors. Go figure.

Apparently "brassiere" is a word no longer in usage. I said it the other day and my grand-daughter cackled. I guess it's just "bra" now.

Here's a word I miss – "percolator." That was just a fun word to say. And what was it replaced with? "Coffeemaker." How dull. Mr. Coffee, I blame you for this.

I miss those made-up marketing words that were meant to sound so modern and now sound so retro. Words like "DynaFlow" and "Electrolux." Introducing the 1963 Admiral TV, now with "Spectra Vision!"

Food for thought - Was there a telethon that wiped out lumbago? Nobody complains of that anymore. Maybe that's what castor oil cured, because I never hear mothers threatening their kids with castor oil anymore.

Some words aren't gone, but are definitely on the endangered list. The one that grieves me most is "supper." (We still have supper each evening! How about you?)

Save a great word. Invite someone to supper. Discuss fender skirts.

"Now also when I am old and grey headed, O God, forsake me not; until I have showed thy strength unto this generation, and thy power to every one that is to come." - Psalm 71:18

GRANDMA'S HANDS

Grandma, some ninety plus years of age, sat feebly on the patio bench. She didn't move, just sat with her head down staring at her hands. When I sat down beside her she didn't acknowledge my presence and the longer I sat I wondered if she was OK. Finally, not really wanting to disturb her but wanting to check on her at the same time, I asked her if she was OK. She raised her head and looked at me and smiled. "Yes, I'm fine, thank you for asking" she said in a clear strong voice.

"I didn't mean to disturb you, grandma, but you were just sitting here staring at your hands and I wanted to make sure you were OK," I explained to her.

"Have you ever looked at your hands?" she asked. "I mean really looked at your hands?" I slowly opened my hands and stared down at them. I turned them over, palms up and then palms down. No, I guess I had never really looked at my hands as I tried to figure out the point she was making.

Grandma smiled and related this story: "Stop and think for a moment about the hands you have, how they have served you well through out your years. These hands, though wrinkled, shriveled and weak have been the tools I have used all my life to reach out and grab and embrace life. They braced and caught my fall when as a toddler I crashed upon the floor. They put food in my mouth and clothes on my back. As a child my mother taught me to fold them in prayer. They tied my shoes and pulled on my boots. They have been dirty, scraped and raw. They were uneasy and clumsy when I tried to hold my newborn son. Decorated with my wedding band they showed the world that I was married and loved someone special. They trembled and shook when I buried my parents and spouse. They have held children, consoled neighbors, and shook in fists of anger when I didn't understand. They have covered my face, combed my hair, and washed and cleansed the rest of my body. They have been sticky and wet, bent and broken. And to this day when not much of anything else of me works real well these hands hold me up, lay me down, and again continue to fold in prayer. These hands are the mark of where I've been and the ruggedness of my life. But more importantly it will be these hands that God will reach out and take when he leads me home. And with my hands He will lift me to His side and there I will use these hands to touch the face of Christ."

I will never look at my hands the same again. But I remember God reached out and took my grandma's hands and led her home. When my hands are hurt or sore or when I stroke the face of my children and husband, I think of grandma. I know she has been stroked and caressed and held by the hands of God. I too, want to touch the face of God and feel his hands upon my face.

"The older he grew, the less he spoke, and the more he said."

EYESIGHT FAILING

An older lady was expecting a gentleman friend to call on her later in the day. She was nervous because her eyesight was failing and was afraid her friend might reject her because she was less than perfect. So, she came up with a plan to prove to him that she could see perfectly. She put a straight pin in a tree that was about 200 feet from her front porch.

When her beau arrived, they sat in the porch swing and were talking when she suddenly stopped the conversation and asked, "Is that a pin sticking in that tree?"

Her friend squinted his eyes and said, "I don't see a thing."

"Well, I'm going to go see," she said as she jumped up, ran toward the tree, and collided with a cow.

"The future is not something we enter. The future is something we create." - Leonard I. Sweet

CURE FOR HICCUPS

A woman went in to a walk-in clinic, where she was seen by a young, new doctor. She was only in the examination room about three minutes when the doctor told her she was pregnant.

She burst out, screaming as she ran down the hall.

An older doctor stopped her and asked what the problem was, and she told him what had happened.

After listening, he had her sit down and relax in another examination room.

The doctor marched down the hallway back to where the first doctor was and demanded, "What's the matter with you? Mrs. Jones is 63 years old, she has four grown children and seven grandchildren, and you told her she was PREGNANT!"

The young doctor continued to write on his clipboard, and without looking up, asked, "Does she still have the hiccups?"

SAVING FOR OLD AGE

After Oliver Wendell Holmes retired at past 90 years of age, his income was reduced. He remarked, "I have always been a prudent man, so this cut in pay will not hurt me; but I am distressed that I cannot continue to lay aside as much as usual for old age!"

"I used to be old and foolish, now I am just old."

HOW TO CALL THE POLICE

George Phillips, an elderly man, from Meridian, Mississippi, was going up to bed, when his wife told him that he'd left the light on in the garden shed, which she could see from the bedroom window. George opened the back door to go turn off the light, but saw that there were people in the shed stealing things.

He phoned the police, who asked "Is someone in your house?"

He said "No, but some people are breaking into my garden shed and stealing from me."

Then the police dispatcher said "All patrols are busy. You should lock your doors and an officer will be along when one is available."

George said, "Okay."

He hung up the phone and counted to 30.

Then he phoned the police again.

"Hello, I just called you a few seconds ago because there were people stealing things from my shed. Well, you don't have to worry about them now because I just shot them."

Within five minutes, six police cars, a SWAT team, a helicopter, two fire trucks, a paramedic, and an ambulance showed up at the Phillips' residence, and caught the burglars red-handed.

One of the Policemen said to George, "I thought you said that you'd shot them!"

George said, "I thought you said there was nobody available!"

THE VALUE OF TIME

To realize the value of one year, ask a student who failed a grade.
To realize the value of one month, ask a mother who gave birth to a premature baby.
To realize the value of one week, as the editor of a weekly newspaper.
To realize the value of one hour, ask the lovers who are waiting to meet.
To realize the value of one minute, ask a person who missed the bus.
To realize the value of one second, ask a person who just avoided an accident.
To realize the value of one millisecond, ask the person who won an Olympic silver medal.

MEASUREMENT OF TIME

Our earthly existence is measured by time. Watches and clocks compute the minutes and the hours. Calendars measure our days, weeks and years. They remind us that our days on earth are numbered.   - Dr. Billy Graham

YOU'RE OVER THE HILL WHEN

You're sitting on a park bench, and a Boy Scout comes up and helps you cross your legs.
Your new easy chair has more options than your car.
One of the throw pillows on your bed is a hot water bottle.
You refer to your $2,500.00 stereo as "the hi-fi."
You run out of breath walking down a flight of stairs.
The waiter asks how you'd like your steak, and you say "pureed."
You frequently find yourself telling people what a loaf of bread used to cost.

"One pleasure of retirement is that you never have to be in a hurry. One of retirement's regrets is wondering why you ever were."

THINGS I HAVE LEARNED

7 Years old: I learned you can't hide broccoli in a glass of milk.

13 Years old: I learned just when I get my room the way I like, Mom makes me clean it up.

24 Years old: I learned that silent company is often more healing than words.

39 Years old: I learned that when someone says something unkind about me, I must live so no one will believe it.

47 Years old: I learned children and grandparents are natural allies.

52 Years old: I learned a vegetable garden is worth more than a cupboard full of pills.

64 Years old: I learned you should not go through life with a catcher's mitt on both hands. You have to be able to throw something back.

72 Years old: I learned that it pays to believe in miracles, and to tell the truth I've seen several.

82 Years old: I learned that even if I have pains, I don't need to be one.

85 Years old: I learned it's important to reach out to people and touch, a hug, a hand shake, or a pat on the back.

92 Years old: I'm learning that I still have a lot to learn.

A SMART AUNT

One of my wife's aunts went to her family physician for an annual check up. Auntie was well into her 80's. Before the doctor left the examining room, he gave her instructions re undressing and putting on a gown. He added, "And maybe you should remove your panties."

Auntie was a sharp cookie with a great sense of humor. She said to her doctor, "I would like for once, to go to a doctor when I did not have to remove my panties."

The doctor also possessed a sense of humor, and with a twinkle in his eye said, "Well I would suggest that you go see an Eye, Ear, Nose & Throat Specialist." - A. Daniel Goldsmith

"Life is what we make it, always has been, always will be." - Grandma Moses

"You're an old-timer if you can remember when rock was something you did in a chair."

CAR COW SALE

A farmer went to town to buy a pickup truck that he saw advertised in the paper for a certain price. He was only a year or so away from retiring from farming and thought he needed to treat himself to one more brand new pick up. After telling the salesman which truck he wanted, they sat down to do the paperwork. The salesman handed the farmer the bill, and the farmer declared, "This is not the price which was listed in the newspaper!" The salesman went on to tell the wise old farmer how he was getting extras such as power brakes, power windows, special tires etc. and that was why the price was increased. The farmer wanted the truck badly, and so he paid the price and drove it home.

A few months later, the salesman called up the farmer and said, "My son is in 4-H and he needs a cow for a project. Do you have any for sale?" The farmer said, "Yes, I have a few cows, and I will sell you one for $500.00. Come have a look at them and take your pick." The salesman said he and his son would be right out. After spending a few hours in the field checking out all the farmer's cows, the two decided on one and the salesman proceeded to write out a check for $500.00.

The farmer said, "Now, wait a minute, that's not the final price of the cow. You're getting extras with it and you have to pay for that too."

"What extras?" asked the salesman.

"Well," said the farmer, "the basic cow is $500.00; two tone exterior is $45.00; extra stomach $75.00; product storing equipment $60.00; straw compartment $120.00; four spigots @ $10.00 each; leather upholstery $125.00; dual horns $45.00; automatic fly swatter $38.00; fertilizer attachment $185.00 for a grand total of $1,233.00."

"An atheist is one who has no invisible means of support."

THE SEVEN AGES OF PEOPLE

1. At twenty work was play, and we kept busy all the day.
2. At thirty we had found our stride, and sailed serenely with the tide.
3. At forty we enjoyed each day and filled the hours a fruitful way.
4. At fifty life was good to her and him, and we looked very fit and trim.
5. At sixty we pressed on with zest, and still resolved to do our best.
6. At seventy we were going strong, and carried in our hearts a song.
7. At eighty we spoke like a sage, and boasted loudly of our age!

"Some people keep you from being lonely when you wish you were."

NAME ALL OF THE STATES

Grandpa asked his grandson how many states there are and if he could name them all. The grandson named all fifty.

"That is wonderful," said the grandparent, I certainly could not have done that when I was your age."

"Yes, and there were only thirteen of them then," commented the grandson.

YOU'VE MIXED MY HOUSE WITH ME

A few short years can't make me old
I feel I'm in my youth
Eternity lies just ahead
A life of joy and truth.

I'm going to live forever there
Life will go on, it'll be grand
You tell me that I'm growing old,
You just don't understand.

The dweller in my little house
Is bright and young, it's me!
I'm starting on a life that lasts
Throughout all eternity.

You only see the outside
Which is all that most folks see
You tell me that I'm growing old,
You've mixed my house with me.

"Age, health, and stage in life have nothing to do with serving or not serving. In each season of life there are attributes and qualities of life and experience that God values in service." - Bruce Kemper

ONE DAY AT A TIME

Someone tried to startle Will Rogers once by asking him what he would do if he had only 48 hours to live. He answered, "I'd live them one at a time." This is one of the most difficult things for us to do, but one of the most profitable. "Take therefore no thought for the morrow; for the morrow shall take thought for the things of itself. Sufficient unto the day is the evil thereof." Matthew 6:34

"One of the privileges of old age is to relate experiences that nobody will believe and give advice that nobody will follow."

ADMIT HE'S WRONG

"Don't count us," said grandma to the officer making a road survey. "We'll be coming back in a few minutes when my husband admits he's going in the wrong direction."

HELP YOURSELF TO THE NUTS

Mrs. Dye had been a faithful member of her local congregation for many years and that is why her absence was noticed. The pastor decided to drop by her house to check up on her after the Sunday service. He knocked on her door and being that she's nearly 85 it took her a bit of time to get to the door.

"Hello, who is it?" she asked.

"It's Pastor Smith", he answered.

"Oh hi-come in, come in, how's the ministry doing?" She said.

"Very well. I just wanted to make sure your prayer needs are being met."

"Oh honey, I haven't felt well lately but I'm getting better."

Just then the phone rang and she excused herself to get it. The pastor sat near a table with an old Reader's Digest and a bowl of peanuts. After 15 minutes, then 20, he heard his stomach growl and began to get restless. He started in on the bowl of peanuts and began reading. After 45 minutes, he suddenly realized that he had eaten all of the peanuts. Right then Mrs. Dye returned and said, "Oh I sure am so sorry, that was my sister from Lowestoft, England. She only calls once a month so when she does we have to catch up on everything."

The pastor feeling a little embarrassed said, "I must also apologize, for while you were gone I got hungry and ate all the peanuts in your little bowl there. Please, forgive me," he said.

Mrs. Dye replied, "Oh that's ok, all I can do anymore is just suck the chocolate off of them!"

OLD TIMERS

Two old timers were discussing a mutual friend. Said one, "Poor old Pete seems to be living in the past."

"And why not?" replied the other. "It's a lot cheaper."

WITH THE CLICK OF THE MOUSE

Twas the night before Christmas and all through the house,
My grandpa was learning with the click of a mouse
Santa came last year on high powered scooter
And gave my dear grandpa, a brand new computer.

"There's a manual with it which tells where to begin,
But first," said Santa, "You must plug the thing in."
The book said "boot it," so computer he kicked
He finally concluded that the mouse must be clicked.

There were so many things that he had to learn,
From start, copy, paste and CD's to burn;
He mastered it all he's a PC geek,
Though not in a day nor even a week.

Now grandpa is writing and reading e-mails,
It's cheaper and faster than the regular mail.
He's dabbled in YouTube, Facebook, and Twitter,
My grandpa worked hard, and he's not a quitter.

So if you have grandpas or friends getting old,
I suggest you write Santa, be polite but be bold;
Ask him this year to get off of his scooter
And give some more grandpas a brand new computer.

What fun they will have as new language they need
To understand software and internet speed;
Abort and retry, and website and crash,
Search engine, database and send to the trash.

Oh yes, they'll be smarter and frustrated too
But day after day, they'll know what to do.
There's Scrabble and Flipwords and many more things,
Like photos and banking, a joke e-mail brings.

Well, I think I'll push start and shut down this rhyme,
I've run out of words and I've run out of time.
I hope that this Christmas when all through the house,
More grandpas are learning by clicking a mouse.
                                    - A. Daniel Goldsmith

"Have a blast while you last."

"I never worry when I get lost. I just change where I want to go."

IT WAS TOUGH IN 1887

Nursing is a lot easier today than it was in 1887. In addition to caring for 50 patients, each nurse was expected to do the following:

1. Daily sweep and mop the floors of your ward, dust the patient's furniture and window sills.
2. Maintain an even temperature in your ward by bringing in a scuttle of coal for the day's business.
3. Light is important to observe the patient's condition. Therefore, each day, fill kerosene lamps, clean chimneys and trim wicks. Wash windows once a week.
4. The nurse's notes are important in aiding the physician's work. Make your pens carefully; you may whittle nibs to your individual taste.
5. Each nurse on day duty will report every day at 7:00am and leave at 8:00pm, except on the Sabbath, on which day you will be off from 12 noon to 2:00pm.
6. Graduate nurses in good standing with the director of nurses will be given an evening off each week for courting purposes or two evenings a week if you go regularly to church.
7. Each nurse should lay aside from each pay day a goodly sum of her earnings for her benefits during her declining years so that she will not become a burden to her family. For example, if you earn $30.00 a month, you should set aside $15.00.
8. Any nurse who smokes, uses liquor in any form, gets her hair done at a beauty shop or frequents dance halls will give the director of nurses good reason to suspect her worth, intentions and integrity.
9. The nurse who performs her labors and serves her patients and doctors without fault for five years will be given an increase of 5 cents a day, providing there are no hospital debts outstanding.

"We are so fond of one another. Our ailments are the same." - J. Swift

COMPLIMENTING THE PASTOR

An elderly saint was seeking to compliment her pastor on his preaching. Unfortunately, it did not come out just right. She said to the pastor, "Pastor your sermons have meant so much to my husband since he lost his mind two years ago."

USHERING DAYS ARE OVER

Our head usher at church had been ushering for over fifty years and should have ceased to do the same a few years ago. He was forever tripping over himself and getting his words mixed up. There was a visitor that had seated herself in someone else' pew. Seeking to help her, he said, "Mardon me padam, you're occupewing the wrong pie. May I sew you to a sheet or would you like a chew in the back of the perch?"

"You grow up the day you have your first real laugh – at yourself."

READING MORE AND DUSTING LESS

I'm reading more and dusting less. I'm sitting in the yard and admiring the view without fussing about the weeds in the garden. I'm spending more time with my family and friends and less time at work whenever possible. Life should be a pattern of experiences to savor, not endure. I'm trying to recognize these moments now and cherish them. I'm not saving anything; I use my good china and crystal for every special event such as losing a pound, getting the sink unstopped, for the first amaryllis bloom. "Someday" and "one of these days" are losing their grip on my vocabulary. If it's worth seeing or hearing or doing, I want to see and hear and do it now. It's those little things left undone that would make me angry if I knew my hours were limited. Angry because I hadn't written certain letters that I intended to write one of these days. Angry and sorry that I didn't tell my wife/husband/significant other/parents often enough how much I truly love them. I'm trying very hard not to put off, hold back or save anything that would add laughter and luster to my life. And every morning when I open my eyes, I tell myself that every day, every minute, every breath is special.

"The most successful person is the one who holds onto the old just as long as it is good and grabs the new just as soon as it is better."
- Robert P. Vanderpool

PRAYER FOR THE DAY

Dear Lord, so far today, God I've done all right. I haven't gossiped, haven't lost my temper, haven't been greedy, grumpy, nasty, selfish or over-indulgent. I'm very thankful for that. But in a few minutes, God, I'm going to get out of bed, and from then on, I'm probably going to need a lot more help. Amen

SO TRUE

Too often we don't realize what we have until it's gone
Too often we wait too late to say, "I'm sorry – I was wrong."
Sometimes it seems we hurt the ones we hold dear to our hearts,
And we allow those foolish things to tear our lives apart.
For too many times we let unimportant things in our minds
And when it's usually too late to see what made us really blind.
So be sure that you let people know how much they mean to you,
Take that time to say the words, before your time on earth is through.
Be sure that you appreciate everything you've got,
And be thankful for the little things in life that mean a lot.

"Imagination was given to man to compensate for what he is not, and a sense of humor to console him for what he is."

I THINK THEY WERE WRONG

"Drill for oil? You mean drill into the ground to try and find oil? You're crazy." - Drillers who Edwin L. Drake tried to enlist for his project to drill for oil in 1859.

"This telephone has too many shortcomings to be seriously considered as a means of communications. The device is inherently of no value to us." - Western Union internal memo, 1876.

"Heavier than air flying machines are impossible." - Lord Kelvin, president, Royal Society, 1895.

"Airplanes are interesting toys but of no military value." - Marechal Ferdinand Foch, Professor of Strategy, Ecole Superieure de Guerre.

"The wireless music box has no imaginable commercial value. Who would pay for a message sent to nobody in particular?" - David Sarnoff's associates in response to his urgings for investment in the radio in the 1920's.

"I think there is a world market for maybe five computers." - Thomas Watson, Chairman of IBM, 1943.

"Man will never reach the moon regardless of all future scientific advances." - Dr. Lee DeForest, inventor of TV.

"Computers in the future may weigh no more than 1.5 tons." - Popular Mechanics, forecasting the relentless march of science, 1949.

"I have traveled the length and breadth of this country and talked with the best people, and I can assure you that data processing is a fad that won't last out the year." - The editor in charge of business books for Prentice Hall, 1957.

"I don't know what use anyone could find for a machine that would make copies of documents. It certainly couldn't be a feasible business by itself." - The head of IBM, refusing to back the idea, forcing the inventor to found Xerox.

"The concept is interesting and well-formed, but in order to earn better than a 'C', the idea must be feasible." - A Yale University management professor in response to Fred Smith's paper proposing reliable overnight delivery service. Smith went on to found Federal Express Corporation.

"We don't like their sound, and guitar music is on the way out." - Decca Recording Co. rejecting the Beatles, 1962.

"640K ought to be enough for anybody." Bill Gates, 1981.

A SMART GRANDSON

When Joshua, our first grandson was born, our daughter, his mother, and our son-in-law lived on the ground floor suite and my wife and I lived upstairs. One summer morning, Joshua came upstairs to see us. It was breakfast time and his mother, who was then expecting her third child, was still in bed. I offered Josh a fresh peach. "No thanks," he said, "Mom said I was not to eat anything upstairs."

"Ah," I said, "Your Mom won't mind. Here Josh, have a nice fresh peach."

"No, Papa, Mom said I was not to eat anything upstairs."

"O.K. if Mom said you were not to eat up here, then we will obey Mom."

After a few seconds of silence, Josh said, "But I could eat it downstairs." So I took Joshua and the peach and went down into their suite and cut up the peach and put some sugar and cream on it and sat with him in their kitchen while he ate the peach downstairs. - A. Daniel Goldsmith

SCHOOL RULES IN THE 1930's & 1940's

In my elementary and high school years the school rules were different. Take for example:
- If you were seen cutting across a neighbor's lawn on your way to or from school, the school monitor, who attended crosswalks, would report you to the principal and you would meet the principal in his office and receive a lecture and a stern warning.
- If you arrived early for school, you had to stay outside in the playground until the bell rang. When the bell rang you then lined up in the basement of the school and marched into class in orderly fashion to a John Phillip Sousa march on an old 78rpm. If you misbehaved while walking into classroom, a teacher who was watching this exercise would call you aside and give you a lecture or more if it was a repeat performance.
- If you were late for school, you sat on the bench outside the principal's office until he met with you and meted out whatever discipline he chose and then sent you off to class.
- If you were caught chewing gum in the classroom, the whole class would watch as the teacher made you walk to the waste basket and deposit your gum and sometimes make you stand in the corner, facing the wall, for as long as the teacher felt was appropriate.
- If you were caught smoking within two blocks of the school campus, you were disciplined by the principal.
- If you failed to do your homework, or were caught talking in class, when you should not have been doing so, you were handed a detention and stayed in after the class was dismissed for one half hour.
- If you really misbehaved and disobeyed the teacher, or were caught swearing or using profanity, the strap was applied where it hurt the most.
  (In case you are wondering, being late for school, and not having homework done were my only two violations). - A. Daniel Goldsmith

MY HUSBAND'S FAVORITE SONG

Her husband died and wanting to honor her husband at his funeral, his wife asked a young man in the choir to sing her husband's favorite song. The young man responded, "I'll be happy to do it. What song do you want me to sing?"

"Jingle Bells."

He looked at her with the most incredulous look. "Are you sure that's what you want me to sing at your husband's funeral?"

"Yes," she confirmed. "That song meant more to him than anything I could ever tell you."

Wondering how he would ever perform this song in such a setting, he decided to say a few words at the beginning to help soften the blow. "You know," he began, "when you love somebody, you'll do anything they ask, even though you don't always know what makes things important in peoples lives. You can't always know the reasons. I loved this man. He was like a mentor to me. His wife has asked me to do something for him, and I want to do it. So I'd like to sing the song that meant more to him than anything that he ever heard in life."

He had already decided that at least the verse would be kept somewhat somber. Thus he began to sing, "Dashing through the snow in a one horse open sleigh." Everybody's head was bowed, and nobody seemed to catch on that this song was really out of context. When he got to the chorus and began to sing, "Jingle Bells, Jingle Bells," the widow's head popped up like somebody had shot her, and her eyes got as big as saucers, and her face got red.

After hearing a couple more phrases, she got up out of her chair, walked up to where the man was singing, put her hand over his mouth, and said to him, "Oh, John, I am so embarrassed. I didn't mean 'Jingle Bells,' I meant 'When They Ring Those Golden Bells'."

PARTY CANCELLED

An ad in the personal ads column of the Everett, WA Herald read: "Dick and Peggy's 50th Anniversary party has been cancelled due to lack of interest. They are now going around the world, courtesy of their children's inheritance."

"Happiness is not a state to arrive at, but a manner of traveling."

METHUSALEH A PENSIONER

Just think, if Methusaleh had retired at 65 and had been receiving a government pension and his company's pension, he would have been a pensioner for 904 years.

"I just celebrated the 40th anniversary of my 50th birthday."
- Art Linkletter

"No one grows old by living, only by losing interest in living."
- Marie Benton Ray

I CAN MANAGE

An older woman was waiting for a bus. She was very large and crippled with arthritis. Her arms were loaded with packages. As the bus door opened, a man waiting behind her offered a helping hand.

The woman smiled and shook her head. "I'd best manage alone," she said. "If I get help today, I'll want it tomorrow."

THE SENIOR'S NEW ALPHABET

A's for arthritis, B's the bad back,
C's the chest pains, perhaps car-di-ac.
D is for dental, decay and decline,
E is for eye sight, can't read that top line.
F is for fissures and fluid retention,
G is for gas which I'd rather not mention.
H is high blood pressure I'd rather it low;
I for incisions with scars you can show.
J is for joints, out of socket, won't mend,
K is for knees that crack when they bend.
L for libido, what happened to sex?
M is for memory, I forget what comes next.
N is neuralgia, in nerves way down low;
O is for osteo, bones that don't grow!
P for prescriptions, I have quite a few,
Just give me a pill and I'll be good as new!
Q is for queasy, is it fatal or flu?
R is for reflux, one meal turns to two.
S sleepless nights and counting my fears,
T for tinnitus and bells in my ears!
U is for urinary; troubles with flow;
V for vertigo, that's 'dizzy,' you know.
W for worry, now what's going 'round?
X is for X-ray, and what might be found.
Y for a new year I'm left here behind,
Z is for zest I still have – in my mind.
I've survived all the symptoms, my body's deployed,
And I'm keeping twenty doctors fully employed.

"Don't simply retire from something; have something to retire to."

I'M OBSOLETE

I never could admit defeat, but now it's clear, I'm obsolete.
When I hear someone say, "dot-com," I don't know where they're coming from.
A mystery that I still don't get is what and where's the internet?
When Larry said he had a mouse, I said, "Well, fumigate the house!"
Am I the only living female, who doesn't understand e-mail?
I always vote and pay my taxes, but I'm not sure just what a fax is.
Nor do I quite know what it means, when people go to church in jeans.
It doesn't matter what we wear, the main thing is that we are there.
Sometimes, I have to tell myself, "You're old. You're ready for the shelf."
But really that's not hard to bear, I'm obsolete, and I don't care.

ON TOP OF OLD FROSTY
(To the tune of "On Top of Old Smoky")

On top of Old Frosty, all covered with fudge
Stand more birthday candles, than a forklift could budge.

No use bein' grouchy, no need feelin' glum,
The tough part is over; the best's yet to come.

Don't lose your old gusto; don't lose your old snap,
Don't stay out till sunrise, you'll sleep through your nap.

Your friends will all love you, and care for you still,
So gee ain't you lucky, you're over the hill!

MY REMEMBERER IS BROKE

My forgetters getting better, but my rememberer is broke,
To you, that may seem funny, but, to me, that is no joke.
For when I'm "here," I'm wondering, if I really should be "there,"
And, when I try to think it through, I haven't got a prayer!

Oft times I walk into a room, say, "What am I here for?"
I wrack my brain, but all in vain, a zero is my score.
At times I put something away, where it is safe, but, gee,
The person it is safest from is generally me!

When shopping, I may see someone, say "Hi" and have a chat,
Then, when the person walks away, I ask myself, "Who's that?"
Yes, my forgetter's getting better, while my rememberer is broke,
And it's driving me plumb crazy, and that isn't any joke.

"Don't spend the last half of your life regretting the first half."

DEAR ABBY

When Abigail Van Buren turned 80, an age when most people have long since retired, she continued to work 8 to 10 hour days on her advice column.

Her advice for aging gracefully: "Fear less, hope more. Eat less, chew more. Talk less, say more. Hate less, love more, and never underestimate the power of forgiveness."

"Why is it that when you retire and time is no longer so important, they give you a watch?"

LIVE TO BE ONE HUNDRED

"How can I live to be a hundred, doctor?" asked the patient.

"Give up cookies, cake and ice cream. Stop eating red meat, potatoes and bread, and no soft drinks," answered the doctor.

"And if I do that, I will live to be one hundred?" asked the patient.

"Maybe not," the doctor said, "but it will certainly seem like it."

✗ "Hair comes in four stages – Bald, Fuss, Is & Was."

HOW TO DEAL WITH TROUBLES

Once John Wesley was walking with a friend whose troubles were really getting him down. He told them all to Wesley, and said sadly, "I can't understand it all. If God is love, why have these things come upon me? It is all too much for me. I can't see through it all."

They were walking in the country, and Wesley noticed a cow looking over a wall. He pointed to it and said: "Why does a cow look over a wall?"

His friend was surprised and with a smile he gave the time-honored answer: "Because it can't see through it."

"Precisely," said Wesley, "and if you can't see through your troubles, try looking over them!"
- Stuart Robertson

"The kind of ancestors we have had is not as important as the kind of descendants our ancestors have."

WHAT IS A GRANDMOTHER

A grandmother is a lady who has no children of her own so she likes other people's little girls. A grandfather is a man grandmother. He goes for walks with the boys and they talk about fishing and tractors and like that.

Grandmas don't have to do anything except be there. They are old so they shouldn't play hard or run. It's enough if they drive us to the supermarket where the pretend horse is, and have lots of dimes ready. Or if they take us for a walk they should slow down past things like pretty leaves or caterpillars. They should never say "Hurry up!" Usually they are fat, but not too fat to tie kid's shoes. They were glasses and funny underwear and they can take their teeth and gums off.

It's better if they don't typewrite or play cards except with us. They don't have to be smart only answer questions like why dogs hate cats or how come God isn't married.

They don't talk baby talk like visitors do because it is hard to understand. When they read to us they don't skip or mind if it is the same story again. Everybody should try to have one, especially if you don't have TV because grandmas are the only grownups who have got time."

- Written by an 8 year old

"Some of us can remember when it cost more to run a car than to park it."

HEARING AID

A gentleman, who was getting on in years, was a bit hard of hearing and did not like to spend his money. One day a friend, seeing a loop of wire hanging over the ear, asked, "Do you have a hearing aid?"

"No," came the answer.

"Then why the wire loop over your ear?"

"It causes people to speak louder," he responded.

WHO'S FAILING

The mind of an elderly lady was beginning to slip, so the family decided it was time for a nursing home. The day after she moved in, her son dropped in to see how she was adjusting and if the move had added to her confusion. He entered the room, and asked her, "Who am I?"

She replied: "Sit down for a minute son, and it will come to you."

"As you go through life, concentrate on the roses not the thorns."

"When saving for old age be sure to lay up a few pleasant memories."

TOO OLD FOR HALLOWEEN

You know that you are too old to "trick or treat"…
- o When you get winded from knocking on the door.
- o When you have to have a kid chew the candy for you.
- o When you ask for high fiber candy.
- o When someone drops a candy bar in your bag and you lose your balance and fall.
- o When people say, "What a Great Boris Karloff mask and you're not wearing a mask.
- o When the door opens and you yell, "Trick or…" and you can't remember the rest.
- o When you have to choose a costume that will not dislodge your hair piece.
- o When you have the only power scooter in the neighborhood.
- o When you have to keep returning home to pee.

"Trim figures is what some people do when they tell their age."

THREE SWIMMING POOLS

An older man who had made a fortune almost overnight was boasting to one of his friends about his new estate with its three swimming pools. "But why three pools?" exclaimed the friend.

"One has cold water," the host replied, "and one has hot water and one has no water at all."

"The one with cold water I can understand. I can even see a reason for the one with hot water," conceded the friend. "But what's the idea of a swimming pool with no water at all?"

"You'd be surprised, Joe," the host confided sadly, "how many of my old friends don't know how to swim."

"Mellow with age, but beware of getting rotten."

RESENT THOSE REMARKS

Joseph E. Atkinson was the publisher of The Toronto Star for 48 years. He consistently supported the Liberal Party of Canada and roused the ire of high ranking Conservatives. In 1947, shortly before he died at the age of 82, the Conservative premier of Ontario, George Drew, denounced Atkinson as an incorrigible liar" and "an evil old man." In his quiet way, Joseph Atkinson was deeply offended as he told a member of Drew's cabinet, "I resent being called old!"

"I have known a great many troubles in my life, but most of them never happened." - Mark Twain

**"Beautiful young people are acts of nature,
beautiful old people are works of art."**

OUR INNOCENT GRANDKIDS

A young child, being very fond of his grandmother, gave her a fist full of dandelions with this note: "These flowers will wilt and die, but you will smell forever." It's the thought that counts.

FORGIVE YOUR ENEMIES

The preacher, in his Sunday sermon, used "Forgive Your Enemies" as his subject.

After a long sermon, he asked how many were willing to forgive their enemies. About half held up their hands. Not satisfied he preached for another ten minutes and repeated his question. This time eighty percent raised their hands. He was still not satisfied and so went on for another ten minutes. All thoughts were now on the Sunday dinner and so everyone lifted their hand except one elderly lady in the rear.

"Mrs. Peters, are you not willing to forgive your enemies?"

"I don't have any."

"Mrs. Peters, that is very unusual. How old are you?"

"Ninety-seven."

"Mrs. Peters, please come up here to the front and tell the congregation how a person can live to ninety-seven and not have any enemies."

The little sweetheart of a lady teetered down the aisle, very slowly turned around & said: "It is very easy. I have outlived them all."

**"At this age and stage of life if you don't wake up
aching in every joint, you are probably dead."**

WHERE DID HE ATTEND SCHOOL

Billy asked his grandfather, "What is a millennium?"

"Don't you know what a millennium is," his grandfather replied. "It's similar to a centennial, only it has more legs."

"Go ahead and mellow with age, but be wary of getting rotten."

GOOD NEWS – BAD NEWS

My grand-daughter came in the house and said "Grandpa, I have good news and bad news."

He said, "I don't want to hear any bad news. I've had a bad day and everything has gone wrong and I can't take anymore bad news. Give me some good news."

"Well, Grandpa," said the grand-daughter, "I want to thank you for letting me use your new car. The good news is that the air-bags work."

FOLLOWING INSTRUCTIONS

Early each morning when I have my first cup of coffee, I usually open the drapes and look out the window and check on the weather. This one morning as I pulled my drapes, I saw my elderly brother jogging by the house. I thought that was unusual because I have hardly ever seen my brother walking, let alone jogging. Well, the next morning I did the same thing and sure enough there he was jogging again. Well, the third day I was expecting to see him jogging again. This time he was skipping. I could take it no longer. I went outside and hollered at Alex and asked him why he was jogging and now skipping.

"Oh," said Alex, "it is my medication. It says to take two days running and then skip a day."

50th WEDDING ANNIVERSARY GIFT

A couple were celebrating their 50th wedding anniversary. This couple had fought and argued for most of the fifty years, so their children got together and agreed upon an anniversary gift. It was a session with a psychiatrist.

Well they argued whether they would accept the gift. They argued over who was going to take them to the psychiatrist. They argued over who was going to sit where in the car. They arrived at the psychiatrist's and continued their arguing and finally argued as to who was going to tell the story.

The psychiatrist was a young fellow, fresh out of university. He decided to do a little shock therapy. He walked over to the woman, put his arms around her and gave her a Hollywood kiss right on the lips. He then turned to the old fellow and said. "Your wife needs this at least three times each week."

"Well," said the husband, "I can bring her in to see you Mondays, Wednesdays and Fridays."

"The best sense of humor belongs to the person who can laugh at himself."

A SURPRISED REACTION

Recovering from a heart attack, George Smith was out having a walk. While he was out, the phone rang. His wife, Betty, answered the phone. It was the Reader's Digest Sweepstake Office informing her that her husband had just won $1,500,000.00. Betty was ecstatic. At long last all of her dreams could be realized. However she remembered that her husband was still recovering from his heart attack and the doctor had said that he should not be exposed to anything that would cause him excitement. So she was fearful of telling her husband this as she was afraid that the shock would give him another heart attack. She pondered what she should do and then decided to call their pastor. He has had a fair bit of experience meeting with people in difficult times. So she phoned the pastor.

"Pastor Ball," she said, "I have a problem and wonder if you would be able to help me."

"Sure," said the pastor, "I'll do what I can. What is your problem?"

"Well, I just had a call from the Reader's Digest Sweepstake Office telling me that George has won $1,500,000.00 and the certified check will be here sometime next week. I'm afraid," she said, "that if I tell George that he might have another heart attack and die."

"I think that I can help you, Betty. I'll be there as soon as I can."

George returned from his walk and the pastor arrived soon after. As they visited, Pastor Ball said to George, "George I have a bit of a problem and need your advice. It is a theoretical question that deals with stewardship. I am wondering what you would say if someone received $1,500,000.00. What would be some good advice re spending the same? Let's assume that you won that amount of money, what would you do?"

"That's easy," said George. "The first thing that I would do would be to give $750,000.00 of it to the church."

Whereupon the pastor had a heart attack and he died.

"You can't see what is ahead when you've got your headlight on the rear bumper." - Dr. Adrian Rogers

LUNCH AT AN ASSISTED LIVING CENTRE

During a visit with a friend at an assisted living centre, I was invited to stay for lunch. As we entered the cafeteria, my friend leaned toward me and whispered, "They have two lines here. We call them 'cane' and 'able'."

"Make peace with your past so it won't screw up the present."
- Regina Brett

"Some people wouldn't ever be completely well, cause then no one would ask them how they are." - L. E. Maxwell

DOCTOR'S ORDERS

Doctor Wiens said to his patient, Mrs. Bradford, "I see that you are over a month late for your appointment. Don't you know that nervous disorders require prompt and regular attention?"

Mrs. Bradford said, "I was just following your orders, Doc."

"Following my orders? What are you talking about? I gave you no such order."

"You certainly did, doctor. You told me to avoid people who irritate me."

"If you're going to be able to look back on something and laugh about it, you might as well laugh about it now." - Marie Osmond

CHURCH SIGN ON A UK CHURCH

As you pass this little church, be sure to plan a visit,
So when at last you're carried in, God won't ask, "Who is it?"

SENIOR PERSONAL ADS

SERENITY NOW: I am into solitude, long walks, sunrises, the ocean and meditation. If you are the silent type, let's get together, take our hearing aids out and enjoy quiet times.

WINNING SMILE: Active grandmother with original teeth seeking a dedicated flosser to share rare steaks, corn on the cob and caramel candy.

MINT CONDITION: Male, 1932, high mileage, good condition, some hair, many new parts including hip, knee, cornea, and valves. Isn't in running condition, but walks well.

MEMORIES: I can usually remember Monday through Thursday. If you can remember Friday, Saturday and Sunday, let's put our two heads together.

THE WIFE DOES THE TALKING

At the close of their 40th wedding anniversary celebration, Esther stood up to thank the family and friends for the lovely evening. In telling the guests how much she enjoyed her forty years with her husband, she said: "I married Henry because he was a military man. He had learned how to cook, sew, make beds and he was in good health. Also he was already used to taking orders."

**"Cultivating a sense of humor
is one of the best ways to stay young."**

A SPECIAL POEM

A row of bottles on my shelf, caused me to analyze myself.
One yellow pill I have to pop, goes to my heart so it won't stop.
A little white one that I take, goes to my hands so they won't shake.
The blue ones that I use a lot, tell me I'm happy when I'm not.
The purple pill goes to my brain, and tells me that I have no pain.
The capsules tell me not to wheeze, or cough or choke or even sneeze.
The red ones smallest of them all, go to my blood so I won't fall.
The orange ones, very big and bright, prevent my leg cramps in the night.
Such an array of brilliant pills, helping to cure all kinds of ills.
But what I'd really like to know, is what tells each one where to go!

**"Years may wrinkle the skin, but to give up interest
wrinkles the soul."** - General Douglas MacArthur

PAPA'S CELL PHONE

When papa left his cell phone at Starbucks after his morning coffee, the clerk scrolled through his saved numbers, stopped at "wife" and pushed send. Nana answered, and the clerk told her what happened.

"Don't worry," said Nana, "I'll take care of it."

A few minutes later, Papa's cell phone rang at Starbucks and the clerk answered it. It was Nana.

"Ernie," she said, "you left your cell phone at Starbucks."

"Laughter is the shock absorber that eases the blows of life."

DON'T GIVE UP HOPE

The retiree was one of those "snow birds" who liked to brag about the number of miles he could drive in one day. As the evening wore on they passed motel after motel with the sign "No Vacancy." Finally, his patient wife said, "I know we'll find a motel soon dear. People are starting to get up."

**"Your mind not only wanders as you get older,
but sometimes it completely leaves you."**

"There is no mother earth, but there is a Father God." - Dr. John Hagee

OVER THE LIMIT

There was an older man driving down the road behind an 18 wheeler. At every stoplight the truck driver would get out of the cab, run back and bang on the trailer door. After seeing this at several intersections in a row the elderly gent followed the trucker until he pulled into a parking lot.

When they both had come to a stop the truck driver once again jumped out and started banging on the trailer door. The older man went up to him and said, "I don't mean to be nosey but I've driven a truck for over 50 years and I've never seen anyone get out and bang on the trailer like you have been doing. Why do you keep banging on that door?"

"Well," said the trucker, "I have 20 tons of canaries and a 10 ton limit, I have to keep half of them in the air all the time!"

"Your outcome in life doesn't depend on your income, but on how you overcome."

100th BIRTHDAY

She bears that quiet dignity, maturity can render;
And bright and warm that eager gaze, her eyes still soft and tender.
And though she's ten times ten, or even twenty-five times four,
She's got her marbles all lined up, and ready for some more.

I must admit my envy, for she's thrice as sharp as I,
And effortlessly sounds my name, though months have slithered by.
I've got a strange suspicion one should never trust her tutor,
I think he's sneaked into her head, one over-sized computer! [8]
- Louise Friesen

"A miser is a weird individual, but makes a great ancestor."

GEORGE BURNS PLAYS TENNIS

George Burns once said, "Tennis is a game for young people. Until age 25, you can play singles. From there until age 35, you should play doubles. I won't tell you my age, but when I played, there were 28 people on the court, just on my side of the net."

"Middle age is that time of life when you can't decide if you have more age or more middle."

THE FLOUR SACK

In that long ago time when things were saved,
When roads were graveled and barrels were staved,
When worn-out clothing was used as rags,
And there were no plastic wrap or bags,
And the well and the pump were way out back,
A versatile item was the flour sack.

Pillsbury's Best, Mother's and Gold Medal too
Stamped their names proudly in purple and blue.
The string sewn on top was pulled and kept,
The flour emptied and spills were swept.
The bag was folded and stored in a sack
That durable practical flour sack.

The sack could be filled with feather and down,
For a pillow, or it would make a sleeping gown.
It could carry a book and be a school bag,
Or become a mail sack slung over a nag.
It made a very convenient pack,
That adaptable cotton flour sack.

Bleached and sewn, it was dutifully worn
As bibs, diapers, or kerchief adorned.
It was made into skirts, blouses and slips
And Mom braided rugs from one hundred strips,
She made ruffled curtains for the house or shack.
From that humble but treasured flour sack!

As a strainer for milk or apple juice,
To wave men in, it was a very good use,
As a sling for a sprained wrist or a break,
To help mother roll up a jelly cake.
As a window shade or to stuff a crack,
We used a sturdy, common flour sack!

As dish towels, embroidered or not,
They covered up dough, helped pass pans so hot,
Tied up dishes for neighbors in need,
And for men out in the field to seed.
They dried dishes from pan, no rack
That absorbent, handy flour sack!

We polished and cleaned stove and table,
Scoured and scrubbed from cellar to gable,
We dusted the bureau and oak bed post,
Made costumes for October, a scary ghost,
And a parachute for a cat named Jack,
From that lowly, useful old flour sack!

So my friends, when they ask you
As curious youngsters often do,
Before plastic wrap, Elmer's Glue
And paper towels, what did you do?
Tell them loudly and with pride don't lack,
"Grandmother had that wonderful flour sack!"
- Colleen B. Hubert

"You can't help getting older, but you don't have to get old."

REPAIR THE COMPUTER

A computer store technician got a call from a senior who had recently purchased her first computer from that store. The senior told the technician that her computer was not working. She described the problem and the technician concluded that her computer needed to be brought in and serviced.

He told her, "Unplug the power cord and bring it up here and I'll fix it for you."

Within the hour, the older woman showed up at the store with the power cord in her right hand.

"By the time you learn all the lessons of life, you're usually too old and too weak to walk to the head of the class."

LATE LEARNER

Ruth Possenti of Havre, Montana was not beyond walking to the head of her class. She was the most mature student in her graduating high school class. The retired bookkeeper, age 86, returned to complete the education she had missed in her youth. Friend and former teacher Mary Granier convinced Possenti to work towards the high school equivalency exams. "It was really her influence that made me think I should do it," said the elderly woman. The real challenge turned out to be physical as she had to struggle up three flights of stairs to reach the classroom. In the end, Possenti aced her final exams. "If I can go back to school at my age then anyone can," she said.

"If you live for the next world, you get this one in the deal. But if you live only for this world, you lose them both." - C. S. Lewis

"A nest is not empty until all of the kids stuff is out of the attic."

A FRUSTRATED GRANDMOTHER

Grandma had hosted a birthday party for seven year old Johnny, one of her grandsons. There were ten of her grandchildren at the party. The party was over and little Johnny asked his grandma if she would help him put on his boots. She could see why. With her pushing and him pulling, she finally managed to get them on his feet. She had worked up a sweat. She almost whimpered when Johnny said, "Grandma, they're on the wrong feet."

She looked, and sure enough, they were. It wasn't any easier pulling the boots off than it was putting them on. She managed to keep her cool as together they worked to get the boots back on – this time on the right feet. He then announced, "These aren't my boots."

She bit her tongue rather than get right in his face and scream, "Why didn't you say so?" like she wanted to. Once again she struggled to help him pull the ill-fitting boots off.

He then said, "They're my brother's boots. My Mom made me wear them."

She didn't know if she should laugh or cry. She mustered up the grace to once again wrestle the boots on his feet again. She then said, "Now, where are your mittens?"

Johnny said, "I stuffed them in the toes of my boots."

**"Birthdays are nice to have, but too many of them
will kill a person."**

BEV SHEA SINGS IN LONDON

During one of the early Billy Graham Crusades in London, England, Bev Shea, the team's soloist, sang a song entitled "It Took A Miracle." One of the lines in the song is "It took a miracle to hang the stars in space…"

After the crusade meeting concluded, an English lady approached Bev and admonished him. She obviously was hard of hearing or did not completely understand Bev's accent, anyhow she said to Bev, "Mr. Shea, you have gone too far!" Bewildered, he asked her what she meant.

She replied, "I know you come from a great country, but you go too far when you sing, "It took America to hang the stars in space."

**"Anxiety does not empty tomorrow of its sorrow,
but only empties today of its strength."**

"Better to be over the hill than under it." - Art Linkletter

✕ MEDICAL CHECK-UP

"Now, Mrs. Lyons," said the doctor, "you say you have shooting pains in your neck, dizziness, and constant nausea. Just for the record, how old are you?"

"Why, I'm going to be 39 on my next birthday," Mrs. Lyons replied indignantly.

"Hmmm," muttered the doctor, "I see that you have a slight loss of memory, too."

"I'm saving that rocker for the day when I feel as old as I really am." - Dwight D. Eisenhower

✕ A HELPFUL PASSENGER

On a recent flight, an elderly passenger kept peering out the window. Since it was totally dark, all she could see was the blinking wing-tip light. Finally, she rang for the flight attendant.

"I'm sorry to bother you," she said, "but I think you should inform the pilot that his left-turn signal light is on and has been for some time."

"You must learn from the mistakes of others, because you can't live long enough to make them all yourself."

PASS ME THAT TOOL, PLEASE

I asked my wife to please pass me a tool. I needed it for some repair work that I was doing. She asked me which tool I wanted. I could not remember what it was called. Frustrated, I finally said "Oh, just read my mind!"

"I am," she replied with a smile, "but I'm drawing a blank."

"Blessed are they who can laugh at themselves for they shall never cease to be amused."

A BAD LEG

An old fellow with a bad leg went to his doctor. The doctor examined him and said, "I can't find a thing wrong. It must be old age."

The man replied: "Doctor, it can't be that. My other leg is the same age, and it's not giving me any pain."

181

THE SENIOR'S CLUB

When our working days are finished, responsibilities diminish
When we're still not stout – but thinnish, we can fish for Bream of Chub.
When with great anticipation, we can plan that long vacation,
And there's time for relaxation, then it's time to join THE CLUB.

Aspirations may be lower, reflexes somewhat slower,
We've more time to use the mower, plant a garden, tend the shrubs.
While the almond tree doth flower, our muscles have less power,
We spend longer in the shower, that's the essence of THE CLUB.

When we yearn for affirmation, as "senior," "elder," statesman,"
We play chess for recreation in the shopping malls, or pub.
But we feel a "second stringer," when rejected as choir singer,
So we then become a "swinger" swiping golf balls with a CLUB.

For our offspring, we are "sitters," persevering, never quitters,
Cleaning up their mess and litters, bathing grandkids in the tub.
Senior condo annexation, means more time for relaxation,
But less income, more taxation so we learn about THE CLUB.

Now it's apposite to mention the political dimension,
Makes it doubtful if your pension will last! Aye there's the rub.
It's certainly not hard to see, that taxes, claw backs, GST
Will shrink your income ruthlessly, that's life, within THE CLUB.

Heights may make us "freaky," while our joints feel stiff and "creaky,"
And the hinges somewhat "squeaky," as worn parts both chafe and rub.
Our faucets seem more leaky, and our vision gets more weaky,
Face and features more antiquey, characteristic of THE CLUB.

Rejecting Zoroastes, wanting good things not life's nasties,
Chapter 12 Ecclesiastes tells God's truth, the real nub;
Of wisdom, what being smart is, helps discover what our part is,
Making sure we know our heart is, firmly anchored in GOD'S CLUB!

Despite some pending horrors, down the road in our tomorrows,
Christ has taken all our sorrows, as our substitute or Sub!
We are glad our destination is not dust but exaltation,
When we join that perfect nation, forever in GOD'S CLUB! [9]
                              - Dr. David Lewis

"Don't major on the minor things in life."

SENIOR GOSSIPERS

Senior gossipers have been cataloged into three different types:

- ➤ The VEST BUTTON type, made up of all those people who seem constantly to be "popping off."
- ➤ The VACUUM CLEANER type, made up of all those people who are always "picking up dirt."
- ➤ The LINIMENT type, made up of those who seem to delight in forever "rubbing it in."

I'M TOO OLD TO DO ANYTHING

Some times "citizens with seniority" (seniors) feel like they don't count any more and that there isn't much that they can do. I have news for you!

Moses was 80 when God called him, and although he cited many excuses, he never mentioned his age.

Socrates gave the world his wisest philosophy at 70

Strauss was still composing serious music after his 80th birthday.

Verdi, at 85, composed the famous "Ave Maria."

Gladstone was still a potential figure in political and intellectual circles when he was 80.

Daniel Webster wrote his monumental dictionary at 70.

Ronald Regan was president of the United States of America when he was in his 70's.

Billy Graham was still preaching as he approached his 90th birthday and Bev Shea, the Billy Graham Crusade soloist, has sung since reaching his 100th.

Don't be too quick to say there's nothing to do. Even if you are bed-ridden, you can still pray.

SENIOR'S PLAYS GOLF

My aunt played a game of golf yesterday with three other retired ladies. At the 16th she hit the ball which headed down the fairway and then hooked to the right, went over some bushes, then over the fence and rolled out on to the highway. Just then a Greyhound Bus was passing by. The front right wheel of the bus hit the golf ball and bounced it back over the fence and the bushes and rolled up on to the greens. One of her friends said, "That was fantastic. How on earth did you do that?"

Auntie replied, "You have to know the bus schedule."

"None are so old as those who have outlived enthusiasm."
- Henry David Thoreau

RETIRING IN PEACE

A wise old gentleman retired and purchased a modest home near a junior high school. He spent the first few weeks of his retirement in peace and contentment. Then a new school year began. The very next afternoon three young boys, full of youthful, after-school enthusiasm, came down his street, beating merrily on every trash can they encountered. The crashing percussion continued day after day, until finally the wise old man decided it was time to take some action.

The next afternoon, he walked out to meet the young percussionists as they banged their way down the street. Stopping them, he said, "You kids are a lot of fun. I like to see you express your exuberance like that. In fact, I used to do the same thing when I was your age. Will you do me a favor? I'll give you each a dollar a day if you'll promise to come around every day and do your thing." The kids were elated and continued to do a bang-up job on the trash cans.

After a few days, the old-timer greeted the kids again, but this time he had a sad smile on his face. "This recession's really putting a big dent in my income," he told them. "From now on, I'll only be able to pay you 50 cents to beat on the cans."
The noisemakers were obviously displeased, but they did accept his offer and continued their afternoon ruckus. A few days later, the wily retiree approached them again as they drummed their way down the street.

"Look," he said, "I haven't received my Social Security check yet, so I'm not going to be able to give you more than 25 cents. Will that be okay?"

"A lousy quarter?" the drum leader exclaimed. "If you think we're going to waste our time, beating these cans around for a quarter, you're nuts! No way, mister. We quit!"

And the old man enjoyed peace.

"I'm not afraid of tomorrow, because I have seen yesterday and I love today."

FANNY CROSBY

Fanny Crosby was blinded when she was six weeks old. She lived into her 90's, composing thousands of beloved hymns. On her 92nd birthday, she cheerfully said, "If in all the world you can find a happier person than I am, do bring him to me. I should like to shake his hand."

"The end of life is not to be happy, nor to achieve pleasure and avoid pain, but to do the will of God, come what may." - Martin Luther King Jr.

"I have held many things in my hands and I have lost them all, but whatever I have placed in God's hands, I still possess." - Martin Luther

"A merry heart maketh a cheerful countenance… He that is of a merry heart hath a continual feast." Proverbs 15:13,15

A THANKSGIVING WISH

May your stuffing be tasty, may your turkey be plump,
May your potatoes and gravy have nary a lump.
May your yams be delicious, may your pies take the prize,
May your holiday dinner stay off of your thighs!

"Our past need not control our present or our future. It is never too late to do what is right, never too late to live our remaining days for God." - Dr. Erwin Lutzer

LATE FOR WORK

After my uncle Ben retired, he managed to secure a job as a greeter at Wal-Mart. Ben had had a problem throughout his life. He was forever late for work. Well, after about ten days of working at Wal-Mart, the manager took my uncle Ben aside and asked, "Do you know what time we start work here at Wal-Mart?"

Uncle Ben replied by saying, "No, sir, I haven't been able to figure it out yet because the rest of the staff is already here when I arrive."

"One nice thing about aging is you can hide your own Easter eggs."

POINTS WORTH PONDERING

Where there's a will, there's a relative.
The older we get the more like ourselves we become.
Remember the best things in life aren't things.
If you don't know where you're going, when you get there you won't know where you are.
A friend is one who knows all about you and likes you anyway.
Old age is when you get it all together, then forget where you put it.

"Live a good, honorable life. Then when you get older and think back, you'll enjoy it a second time.

GOVERNMENT OFFICIAL IS ABOVE THE LAW

A cocky Department of Agriculture representative stopped at a farm and talked with the old farmer; "I need to inspect your farm."

The old farmer said, "You're welcome anywhere on my land, but you had better not go into that field."

The Agriculture representative said in a wise tone of voice, "I have the authority of the U. S. Government with me. See this card, I am allowed to go wherever I wish on agricultural land."

So the old farmer went about his farm chores. Later, the farmer heard loud screams and saw the Department of Agriculture man running for the fence. Close behind him was the farmer's prize bull. The bull was madder than a nest full of hornets, and the bull was gaining at every step.

"Help," the representative shouted to the farmer, "What should I do?" he screamed helplessly.

The old farmer, hooking his thumbs in his overalls, called out, "Show him your card!"

"Some people try to turn back their odometers. Not me, I want people to know why I look this way. I've traveled a long way and some of the roads weren't paved."

A GEOGRAPHY LESSON

My old neighbor was not pleased with the way his barber had been cutting his hair and so decided to seek out a hairdresser. He went across town to a hairdresser that had been recommended to him. The hairdresser noticed his accent and asked where he was from. He responded by telling her that he was from Trinidad.

"Oh," she said, "is that in Arabia?"

"No," he said, "it is in the Caribbean."

She laughed, "Sorry," she said, "I never was very good at geometry."

MAKES GOOD SENSE

An 83 year old woman talked herself out of a speeding ticket by telling the young officer that she had to get there before she forgot where she was going. Makes good sense!

"God gave women a sense of humor so they could understand the jokes they married."

"Don't worry if your life is hard and your rewards are few, remember the mighty oak was once a nut like you."

VISITING THE KIDS

One of the most invigorating aspects of reaching old age is the anticipation you feel as your children set about establishing nests of their own. Sure, Ramona and I are experiencing the customary jolts of nostalgia as we remember the house as it once was: Noisy. Messy. Cloudy with a chance of incoming mud. But I can scarcely contain my excitement. They are flying from the nest. And I will soon have the opportunity to visit their homes. Here are just a few of the activities I have planned, should they choose to have us over for the weekend.

❖ Show up and announce, "I brought some friends. What's for supper?"
❖ Leave taps dripping, lights blazing, and an open mayo jar on the counter overnight.
❖ Replace Michael Buble CDs with something from The Gaithers.
❖ Use their phone to cal friends in Singapore.
❖ Crack the fridge door open for the night.
❖ Gather wrenches and bury them (the wrenches, not the kids) in the sandbox.
❖ Beat the wooden furniture with pillows until the stuffing is gone.
❖ Invite six friends over about 10 PM. Say, "Go ahead and make yourselves sandwiches."
❖ Take everyone out for dinner and forget my wallet. [10]

- Phil Callaway

"When saving for old age be sure to lay up a few pleasant memories."

POUND FOR POUND

For many years a baker in a little country town bought the butter that he used for his baking from a nearby farmer. One day the baker suspected that the bricks of butter were not full pounds, and for several days he weighed each pound of butter. He was right. The pounds of butter were less than a pound and he had the farmer arrested.

At the trial the judge said to the farmer, "I presume that you have scales?"

"No, your honor."

"Then how do you manage to weight the butter that you sell?" inquired the judge.

The farmer replied, "That's easily explained, your honor. I have balances and for a weight I use a one pound loaf of bread that I buy from the baker."

"Pack up your gloomies in a great big box, then sit on the lid and laugh." - Barbara Johnson

THOUGHTS ON AGING

One of the most disturbing aspects of aging is my growing inability to recall important information like the Greek alphabet, the greatest export of China, and where I left my glasses.

This becomes particularly pronounced when I go upstairs to get something. Halfway up I realize I have no inkling of what it is I am going upstairs to get. Should I go downstairs and try to remember what it was I needed? Unable to decide, I resort to sitting on the landing, only to discover after three minutes that I have completely forgotten whether I was originally upstairs coming down or downstairs going up.

Some of us think growing old is simply an unavoidable process that begins at birth while others search for the right medicine to help cope with this age old syndrome. I think that the older people who enjoy a sense of humor may have found the best medicine of all.

"Seniors are funny. They want the front of the bus, the middle of the road, and the back of the church."

STOP 'CHOPIN' YOUR WORDS

I was trying to get my teenage grand-daughter to stop dropping the "g's" in words like walkin, goin, seein, etc. Apparently I was doing a good job. One day the phone rang and my grand-daughter answered. "It's for you, grandma. The lady says she is your cousing."

REMEMBER WHEN

Decisions were made by going "eeny-meeny-miney-mo?"
Mistakes were corrected by simply exclaiming, "Do over?"
"Race issue" meant arguing about who ran the fastest?
Money issues were handled by whoever was the banker in Monopoly?
Catching the fireflies could happily occupy an entire evening?
Being old, referred to anyone over 30?
It was magic when dad would "remove" his thumb or "take" your nose?
Having a weapon in school meant being caught with a slingshot?
Nobody was prettier than mom?
A foot of snow was a dream come true?
Scrapes and bruises were kissed and made better?
Spinning around, getting dizzy and falling down was cause for giggles?
Water balloons were the ultimate weapon?

"Genuine humor is always kindly and gracious. It points out the Weakness of humanity, but shows no contempt and leaves no sting."

A SEVENTEENTH CENTURY NUN'S PRAYER

Lord, Thou knowest better than I myself know that I am growing older and will some day be old. Keep me from the fatal habit of thinking I must say something on every subject and on every occasion. Release me from the craving to straighten out everybody's affairs. Make me thoughtful, but not moody; helpful, but not bossy. With my vast store of wisdom it seems a pity not to use it all, but Thou knowest, O Lord, that I want a few friends at the end. Keep my mind free from the recital of endless details; give me wings to get to the point. Seal my lips on my aches and pains. They are increasing, and love of rehearsing them is becoming sweeter as the days go by.

I dare not ask for grace enough to enjoy the tales of others' pains, but help me to endure them with patience. I dare not ask for an improved memory, but for a growing humility and a lessening cocksureness when my memory seems to clash with the memories of others. Teach me the glorious lesson that occasionally I may be mistaken. Keep me reasonably sweet; I do not want to be a saint, some of them are so hard to live with, but a sour old person is one of the crowning works of the devil. Give me the ability to see good things in unexpected places, and talents in unexpected people. And give me, O Lord, the grace to tell them so. Amen.

"Hem your day with prayer and it will be less apt to unravel at the edges."

INSPIRED BY JOHN WESLEY

When John Wesley was an old man, a striking testimony was borne to the radiance of his personality. It has been said that wherever he went he radiated a great sense of happiness. In him, old age appeared delightful, like an evening without a cloud. It was impossible to observe him without wishing that your latter days would be like his.

WHAT DO YOU LIVE FOR

The psychologist William Moulton Marston asked three thousand persons, "What do you have to live for?" He was shocked to find that 94 percent were simply enduring the present while they waited for the future; waited for "something" to happen; waited for children to grow up and leave home; waited for next year; waited for another time to take a long dreamed-about trip; waited for someone to die; waited for tomorrow without realizing that all anyone ever has is today because yesterday is gone and tomorrow never comes. - Douglas Lurton

"Give your entire attention to what God is doing right now, and don't get worked up about what may or may not happen tomorrow. God will help you deal with whatever hard things come up when the time comes." [11]

INTERVIEWED MY FATHER

In the spring of 1997, I interviewed my father for a senior's quarterly paper which I edited. Among the several questions which I asked him, one question was this: "What advice would you give to your peers? There are several who will read this who are in their 70's or 80's and some in their 90's. Do you have anything to say to them?"

Dad was 88 years old at the time of the interview. This was his answer to my question: "Keep active. Whatever you have been doing in life, keep doing it. You don't have to quit just because you retired. You only change positions. Your pay check comes from a different source. I didn't stop studying. I'm still studying. I'm still reading, (in answer to another question he said that he reads a lot. He reads through the Bible once a year and he reads two or three books each month). I still try to help people and encourage them. I want to keep doing so long as I have the health, strength, and mind." - A. Daniel Goldsmith

LEARNING FROM CENTENARIANS

The McIntosh Church Growth Network shared some habits of those reaching their one hundred year birthday. Here are some of the thoughts from the MCGN findings.

People who reach their 100th birthday stay mentally active. They keep learning. They are continually looking for experiences where they can learn something new, music lessons, a new language, travel, etc.

The most frequent reason given by centenarians for their long life is hard work. Only 3.5% of centenarians retired at age 65. Rather than being workaholics who worked compulsively without pleasure, successful agers worked hard because they enjoyed it.

Twelve hundred centenarians were interviewed and 96% of them had their days organized and well structured. Nearly all of them got up, ate, exercised, read, worked, and went to bed according to a regular schedule.

One hundred year olds help others. According to the MCGN report, many work with organizations such as the PTA, Boy and Girl Scouts, church, historical societies, libraries, etc.

People who live to 100 and beyond continue to live their passion. It does not matter what they are interested in as long as they are passionate about some activity which gives them a vision.

Most people who live 100 years have suffered their share of losses. They are characterized by a resilience to put their life back together after it has fallen apart.

The seventh trait which MCGN pointed out relative to the centenarian is that many of them stay focused on God. Growing medical evidence appears to point to a correlation between physical health and belief in God. [12]

"To be anxious about nothing, pray about everything."

THANK YOU LORD

Thank You Lord for the alarm that rang this morning and rudely awakened me from a comfortable sleep. Thank You Lord that I have ears that hear. Many people are deaf.

Thank You Lord that I had the strength to rise from my bed. Many people have no bed and then there are many that have been bedridden for years.

Thank You Lord that I had a place where I could freshen up. I was able to stand beneath the shower head and feel the warm water run down my body. Many people are dying with thirst. They have little or no water. I have an abundance of water.

Thank You Lord, that even though I have my aches and pains, I was able to walk to the kitchen table. Many have no table and many cannot walk.

Thank You Lord that I had food on that table. It didn't look like a fine dining restaurant, but I had ample food and more in the cupboard. Many are hungry and starving.

Thank You Lord that I was awakened from my afternoon nap when my daughter phoned. Thank You Lord that I have family that cares enough to phone me. Many are forgotten by their family. Their children no longer call.

Thank You Lord that many years ago I heard the message that You loved me and paid the supreme sacrifice for my sin, and that I responded in faith and received You as my Lord and Savior. Many have never ever heard the sweet gospel story and do not know a personal relationship with God.

Thank You Lord for the freedom of worship and for my church, a place where I can worship You and enjoy the fellowship of fellow believers. Many are deprived this freedom and privilege.

Thank You Lord, that when this day is done, and I am worn and weary, that I have a place that I call home and where I will be able to rest and renew my strength. Many are homeless. They have no place that they can call home.

Thank You Lord, that when I die, I know where I am going. Do you?
- A. Daniel Goldsmith

PRAYING WHEN IN PAIN

Dear Lord, please grant that I shall never waste my pain, for to fail without learning, to fall without getting up, to sin without overcoming, to be hurt without forgiving, to be discontent without improving, to be crushed without becoming more caring, to suffer without growing more sensitive, makes of suffering a senseless, futile exercise, a tragic loss, and of pain the greatest waste of all.
- Dick Innes

GREATEST LESSON EVER LEARNED

A church in Atlanta, Georgia was honoring a 92 year old former senior pastor who had been retired for many years. After a warm welcome and the applause had quieted down, the elderly pastor rose from his chair and walked slowly to the podium. Without a note of any kind he placed both hands on the pulpit to steady himself and then quietly and slowly began to speak.

"When I was asked to come here today and say a few words, your pastor asked me to tell you what was the greatest lesson that I had learned in my years of preaching. I thought about it for a few days and boiled it down to just one thing that I could always rely on when tears and heartbreak and pain and fear and sorrow paralyzed me… the one thing that would comfort was this verse…

"Jesus loves me this I know
For the Bible tells me so,
Little ones to Him belong,
They are weak but He is strong,
Yes, Jesus loves me..."

When he finished, the church was quiet. You actually could hear his foot steps as he shuffled back to his chair.

SENIOR VERSION OF JESUS LOVES ME

Jesus loves me, this I know,
Though my hair is white as snow
Though my sight is growing dim,
Still He bids me trust in Him.

Yes, Jesus loves me, Yes, Jesus loves me,
Yes, Jesus loves me, the Bible tells me so.

When the nights are dark and long,
In my heart He puts a song,
Telling me in words so clear,
"Have no fear, for I am near."

When my work on earth is done,
And life's victories have been won,
He will take me home above,
Then I'll understand His love.

I love Jesus does He know?
Have I ever told Him so?
Jesus loves to hear me say,
That I love Him every day.

DO YOU KNOW WHERE YOU'RE GOING

Albert Einstein, a theoretical physicist who was widely regarded as the greatest scientist of the 20th century, was traveling on a train. The conductor was collecting the tickets. When he came to Mr. Einstein, Einstein looked in his pocket, he looked in his brief case, and he looked everywhere but could not find his ticket. The conductor said, "Mr. Einstein, I know who you are and I know that you would have purchased a ticket. Don't worry about it."

The conductor walked on. When he got to the end of the car, he turned around and looked back and there was Einstein down on his hands and knees still looking for his ticket. The conductor walked back and said, "Mr. Einstein I told you not to worry about your ticket. I know you and I know that you would have purchased a ticket."

Albert Einstein said to the conductor, "I know who I am and I know that I bought a ticket, but I'm trying to find my ticket because I don't know where I am going."

I KNOW WHO I AM AND I KNOW WHERE I'M GOING. My ticket to heaven was paid for when the Lord Jesus Christ shed His blood on Calvary. I reached out in faith and received Him as my personal Lord and Savior. DO YOU KNOW WHERE YOU'RE GOING?

"Jesus is preparing a place for us and preparing us for that place."

BEAUTIFUL NEW HOMES TO BE GIVEN AWAY

- Located in a perfect city
- Workmanship guaranteed
- No utility bills.
- A perfect neighborhood
- No racism
- No locks or alarm system needed
- No vandalism
- No leaky roofs
- Termite free
- Immaculate streets and landscaping
- A variety of fruit trees
- Crystal clear waters nearby
- Free transportation everywhere
- Moving expenses fully paid by the Designer
- Apply for your home today

Jesus said: "He that comes to me I will not cast out." John 6:37
Jesus said: "I go to prepare a place for you…" John 14:2

**"You can get your grandchildren off of your lap,
but you never get them out of your heart.**

THE BRIDGE BUILDER

An old couple going a lone highway,
Came at the evening, cold and gray,
To a chasm vast and wide and steep,
With waters rolling cold and deep.
The old couple crossed in the twilight dim,
The sullen stream had no fears for them,
But they turned, when safe, to the other side,
And built a bridge to span the tide.
"Old couple," said a fellow pilgrim near,
"You are wasting your strength with building here,
Your journey will end with the ending day,
You never again will pass this way.
You've crossed the chasm, deep and wide,
Why build you this bridge at eventide?"
The builders lifted their old gray heads,
"Good friend, in the path we have come," they said
"There followeth after us today
A youth whose feet must pass this way.
The chasm that was as naught for me,
To that fair-haired youth may a pitfall be,
He, too, must cross in the twilight dim,
Good friend, we are building this bridge for him."
- Will Allen Dromgoole

BILLY SUNDAY FIGHTS SIN

It is said that Billy Sunday, the baseball evangelist and reformer never spared himself or his vigorous attacks on sin. He thundered against evil from the "Gay Nineties" through the "Great Depression." He preached Christ as the only answer to man's needs until his death in 1935.

"I'm against sin," he said. "I'll kick it as long as I've got a foot, and I'll fight it as long as I've got a fist. I'll butt it as long as I've got a head. I'll bite it as long as I've got a tooth. When I'm old and fistless, and footless and toothless, I'll gum it till I go home to Glory and it goes home to perdition."

**"I am intensely interested in the future as I expect
to spend most of my life there."**

"For the child of God, death is not the end but merely the door into a higher and more exalted life of intimate contact with Christ."
- Phillip Keller

I WIN FOR BOTH WORLDS

Before the home going of Dr. Bob Jones, Sr., founder of Bob Jones University, Greenville, SC, he gave the following testimony concerning his precious mother.

"When I was fourteen years old, I knelt by my dying mother's bed. She smiled at me through the death shadow on her face and said she was going Home and asked me to meet her in Heaven. I gave her my promise.

Her body sleeps now in a lonely cemetery in the state of Alabama. As I have sat by her grave and listened to a funeral dirge played by the wind in the pine trees nearby, I have said, 'Mother, I will see you again someday.'

Some people say I am dreaming. If I am, do not wake me. If this world were all, I would still want my Christian faith. My faith hangs a rainbow of hope over the dust of my dead and kindles a smile on the brow of my bereavement.

This world is not all. There is a God! There is a Heaven! There is a Hell! I am playing a safe game. If there were only one world, I have already won. Since there is an afterlife, I win for both worlds. You do not have to take any chances with your soul. Do not take any!"

"Going to church doesn't make you a Christian any more than going into a garage makes you an automobile." - Evangelist Billy Sunday

MONEY CAN BUY

A bed but not sleep. Books but not brains.
Food but not appetite. Finery but not beauty.
A house but not a home. Medicine but not health.
Luxuries but not culture. Amusement but not happiness.
A crucifix but not a Savior. A church pew but not heaven.

MY DESIRE

The desire of my heart is so to live,
That people will say as I pass,
Not what a wonderful Christian he is,
But a wonderful Christ that he has.

"Live each day as though it were your last, it may be."

OLD AGE

The sunny side of seventy! I've reached it long ago,
And now I'm nearing eighty, with hair as white as snow,

Eyes dim, joints still, back feeble – I seem an evil case
To sing of sunny seventy seems somewhat out of place,

But is it? Pause and ponder what the good Book has said
Of righteousness and glory crowning the hoary head.

Think of the rocks and quick sands which I have safely passed
By the Good Shepherd's guidance through many a roaring blast.

Now I am near the borders of the bright shining land
Where blessed saints are waiting for me to join their band

For me, all believers cleansed in that marv'lous flood
Which frees from all defilement, e'en Christ's atoning blood.

Does not that counterbalance the weakness of my frame?
Oh, how the thought of glory has set my heart on flame!

What though this mortal body, poor tenement of clay,
'Neath death's dominion falling, should perish and decay?

What matters? All is brightness, for thus proclaims the Word
Absent from this poor body, then present with the Lord.

How glorious are my prospects, Lo! to faith's piercing view
Lie realms of brightest glory, scenes ever fair and new,

Where Christ in heavenly glory, the Lamb of God divine,
God's Son, His well-beloved, doth reign, and Christ is mine.
- Hector Maiben

NEVER LOST THE WONDER

Gypsy Smith was a great English evangelist who began his preaching in 1877 at the age of 17. He said, "I was born in a field. Don't put me in a flowerpot." Gypsy Smith used to say that he did not know any more about theology than a jack rabbit knew about ping-pong. He was a simple, colorful and original preacher.

Smith was asked the secret of his freshness and vigor, even into his old age. He simply replied, "I have never lost the wonder." He had a child's heart and never lost the wonder.

THE WONDERER

I wish that I could understand, the moving marvel of my Hand;
I watch my fingers turn and twist, the apple bending of my wrist.

The dainty touch of finger-tip, the steel intensity of grip;
A tool of exquisite design, with pride I think, "It's mine! It's mine!"

Then there's the wonder of my Eyes, where hills and houses, seas and skies
In waves of light converge and pass, and print themselves as on a glass.

Line, form and color live in me, I am the beauty that I see.
Ah! I could write a book of size, about the wonder of my Eyes.

What of the wonder of my Heart, that plays so faithfully its part?
I hear it running sound and sweet; it does not seem to miss a beat;

Between the cradle and the grave it never falters, stanch and brave.
Alas! I wish I had the art to tell the wonder of my Heart.

Then oh! But how can I explain the wondrous wonder of my Brain?
That marvelous machine that brings all consciousness of wonderings;

That lets me from myself leap out and watch my body walk about;
It's hopeless, all my words are vain to tell the wonder of my Brain.

That I myself would glorify, you're just as wonderful as I,
And all creation in our view is quite as marvelous as you.

Come, let us on the sea-shore stand, and wonder at a grain of sand;
And then into the meadow pass, and marvel at a blade of grass;

Or cast our vision high and far and thrill with wonder at a star;
A host of stars, night's holy tent, huge-glittering with wonderment.

If wonder is in great and small, then what of Him who made it all?
In Eyes and Brain and Heart and Limb, let's see the wondrous work of Him.

In house and hill and sward and sea, in bird and beast and flower and tree,
In everything from sun to sod, the wonder and the awe of God.
- Robert W. Service

"God whispers to us in our joys, speaks to us in our difficulties, and shouts to us in our pain." - C. S. Lewis

OUR FINAL SIGH AND FUTURE SONG

Lord, we live each breath, each day,
Knowing that final sigh will come
When in Your way you call us home
Bursting the bonds of flesh and bone.

Then the petty things of life,
The clothes we wear the food we eat
The places we go and the goods we seek
Will seem so small, when You we meet!

Then our hearts will burst in song
Finally free from earth's strong bond
Our spirits rise to join that throng
Of blood-washed sinners, cleansed of wrong!

And then for all eternity
We'll join transformed humanity
Our final fulfillment in Christ we'll see
Bowing before His Majesty.

Hallelujah! Let It Be!
Free at last....so truly free! [13]
- Jack Chapin

"He who provides for this life, but takes no care for eternity, is wise for a moment, but a fool forever."

ONLY ONE LIFE

Only one life twill soon be past, only what's done for Christ will last.
Only one need both night and day, only to trust and watch and pray.
Only one faith steadfast and sure, only in God is man secure.
Only one love sublime and true, only one Christ who cares for you.
Only His Word of truth and right, ever shall be my guiding light.
Only one guide His paths are right, only one road of peace and light.
Only one law of life for all, keep His commandments, obey His call.
Only to live and faithful be, only to hope and trust in Thee.
Only one way, one Shepherd, too, only our Lord will see us through.
Only one place that's safe to be, only God's hand to cover me.
Only one thing to do in me, only seek God for He will lead.
Only one cure for sinfulness, only His love our souls to bless.

THE TWENTY-THIRD PSALM

The Lord is my shepherd and giveth to me
All that I needeth whatever it be;
All pastures so green, and all waters so still,
He giveth abundance; my soul He doth fill.

He guideth my footsteps for righteousness sake
Through mountains or valleys lest sorrow o'er take;
No evil will harm me when my Lord is near;
His rod and His staff are my joy and my cheer.

He sets me a table in front of my foes;
Anoints me with oil from my head to my toes;
I'll live in His fold all the length of my days,
Where goodness and mercy shall be all His praise. [14]
- Clifford A. Olson

"Man's way leads to a hopeless end. God's way leads to an endless hope.

DEFINITION OF A CHRISTIAN

He has a mind and knows it. He has a will and shows it. He sees his way and goes it. He draws a line and toes it. He has a chance and takes it. Sees a friendly hand and shakes it. Knows a rule and never breaks it. If there is no time, he makes it. He loves the truth, stands by it, nor ever tries to shy it. He owes a debt and pays it. He sees the path Christ trod and for strength grips the hand of God.

"Christians may not see eye-to-eye, but they can still walk arm-in-arm."

WHAT IS A SAINT

Rev. David Ogilvie asked the children during the story time at church if any of them knew what a saint was. The children were silent. "Do you know anything at all about saints?" he asked.

One young boy finally raised his hand. "Well," he said, "they go marching in."

BEYOND EARTH

Beyond earth's sorrows, the joy of heaven; beyond earth's shadows, a glorious dawn.
Beyond earth's battles, sweet peace unending; beyond earth's sunsets, in heaven's morn.

**"I've read the last page of the Bible.
It's all going to turn out all right."** - Dr. Billy Graham

THE GOSPEL TRAIN

My neighbor missed a train today
His mind was sorely tried
He really had to catch that train
A relative had died.

Some cause or something kept him late
To miss train fifty six
He was to be a bearer, now
He's in a pretty fix.

Untold numbers miss the train
On which they were to travel
Myriad causes why so late
Many reasons they unravel.

But behold a train we must not miss
The fare now paid for all,
Christ paid our fares upon the cross,
Pray let us heed the call.

Then all aboard the Gospel train,
For destination heaven
Get in touch with heaven now
Our Christ, whose side was riven.

Jesus is pilot of the train
Our Savior, we adore
If we can get aboard through Him
We are safe for evermore.

Come, make our reservations now
Our Pilot is so kind,
Don't put it off till it's too late
And then be left behind.
                    - Ed Worth

"The duties of Godly grandparenthood falls into four roles: Giving a blessing; Leaving a legacy; Bearing a torch, and Setting a standard."
                    - Dr. Tim Kimmel

WHAT THEN

When the great factory-plants of our cities
Have turned out their last finished works,
When our merchants have sold their last products,
And sent home the last of the clerks;
When our banks have transacted their business,
And paid out the last dividend;
When the Judge of the earth calls a reckoning,
And asks for a balance – WHAT THEN?

When the church choir has sung its last anthem,
And the preacher has made his last prayer;
When the people have heard their last sermon,
And the sound has died out on the air;
When the Bible lies closed on the pulpit,
And the pews are all empty of men,
When each one stands facing his record,
And the great book is opened – WHAT THEN?

When the actors have played their last drama,
And the mimic has made his last fund,
When the film has flashed its last picture,
And the billboard displayed its last run;
When the crowds seeking pleasure have vanished,
And gone out in the darkness again,
When the trumpet of ages is sounded,
And we all stand before Him – WHAT THEN?

When the bugle call sinks into silence,
And the long marching columns stand still;
When the captain repeats his last orders,
And they've captured the last fort and hill;
When the flag has been hauled from the mast-head,
And peace seems to reign among men,
When those who rejected the Savior
Are asked for a reason – WHAT THEN?

END LIFE WELL

My life on earth will end, what day I cannot tell;
My one desire and prayer is that I will end it well.
- A. Daniel Goldsmith

"When God gets ready for you, you better be ready for Him."

I AM STILL WITH THEE

After an extended illness, a Christian woman was taken to the hospital for surgery. Noticing her distress as she was being prepared for the operation, an attendant took her hand and whispered softly, "Madam, you have nothing to fear. Only one of two things could possibly happen to you, and both of them are good. If you should die, you will be with Jesus. If you should live, Jesus will be with you. In either case, both of you will be together.

A PLACE CALLED HEAVEN

Dr. Charles E. Fuller, who for many years conducted The Old Fashioned Revival Hour from the Long Beach Municipal Auditorium in Long Beach, California announced one Sunday that he would be speaking the following Sunday on the subject of heaven. During that week a beautiful letter was received from an old man who was very ill. The following is a part of that letter:

"Next Sunday you are to talk about Heaven. I am interested in that land because I have held a clear title to a bit of property there for over fifty-five years. I did not buy it. It was given to me without money and without price. But the Donor purchased it for me a tremendous sacrifice. I am not holding it for speculation since the title is not transferable. It is not a vacant lot.

For more than half a century I have been sending materials out of which the greatest Architect and Builder of the Universe has been building a home for me which will never need to be remodeled nor repaired because it will suit me perfectly, individually, and will never grow old.

Termites can never undermine its foundations for they rest on the Rock of Ages. Fire cannot destroy it. Floods cannot wash it away. No locks nor bolts will ever be placed upon its doors, for no vicious person can ever enter that land where my dwelling stands, now almost completed and almost ready for me to enter in and abide in peace eternally, without fear of being ejected.

There is a valley of deep shadow between the place where I live in California and that to which I shall journey in a very short time. I cannot reach my home in that City of Gold without passing through this valley of shadow. But I am not afraid because the best Friend I ever had went through the same valley long, long ago and drove away all its gloom.

He has stuck by me through thick and thin, since we first became acquainted fifty five years ago, and I hold His promise in printed form never to forsake me or leave me alone. He will be with me as I walk through the valley of shadow, and I shall not lose my way when He is with me.

I hope to hear your sermon on Heaven next Sunday from my home in Los Angeles, California, but I have no assurance that I shall be able to do so. My ticket to heaven has no date marked for the journey, no return coupon and no permit for baggage. Yes, I am all ready to go and I may not be here while you are talking next Sunday evening, but I shall meet you there some day.

"Heaven is a prepared place for a prepared people."

202

LIFE BEYOND THE GRAVE

If you're awake before you die
I trust you will have made,
The preparations for your life
Your life beyond the grave.

Don't take a chance for you must choose
Your life beyond the grave,
Decide today, oh do not lose,
The Truth, the Life, the Way.

God's only Son, He is the One
For life beyond the grave,
Trust Him today, ere day is done,
And be eternally saved.
- A. Daniel Goldsmith

CHRISTMAS IN HEAVEN

I've had my first Christmas in heaven, a glorious, wonderful day!
I stood with saints of the ages, who found Christ, the Truth and the Way.

I sang with the heavenly choir; just think! I, who loved so to sing,
And oh, what celestial music, we brought to our Savior and King.

We sang the glad songs of redemption, of how Jesus to Bethlehem came,
And of how they called His name Jesus, that all might be saved through His name.

We sang once again with the angels, the song that they sang that blest morn,
When shepherds first heard the glad story, that Jesus, the Savior, was born.

Oh, darling, I wish you had been here; no Christmas on earth could compare,
With all the rapture and glory we witnessed in heaven so fair.

You know how I always loved Christmas, it seemed such a wonderful day,
With all of my loved ones around me, the children so happy at play.

Yes, now I can see why I loved it, and oh, what a joy it will be,
When you and my loved ones are with me, to share in the glories I see.

So, dear ones on earth, here's my greeting; look up till the day dawn appears,
And oh, what a Christmas awaits us beyond all our partings and tears!
- Dr. Albert Simpson Reitz

"When we confess our sins, God casts them into the deepest ocean, then God places a sign out there that says 'No fishing allowed'!" - Corrie ten Boom

HAVE YOU REALLY HEARD?

When we were children, many of us had frustrated parents who asked us if we had really heard their reminder to finish an unwanted chore. We may have claimed to have heard, but our attitude and actions said otherwise.

As you think about your own response to the gospel, have you *heard* it? If so, how have you responded to it? It's easy to put off making a decision. And this becomes an even greater tendency when eternal consequences are at stake. But God wants us to make a decision about His Son.

The gospel is a simple but heart-penetrating truth. The Bible tells us that all have sinned and fallen short of God's perfect standard of righteousness (Rom. 3:23). The terrible consequence of this is that we are separated from a holy God (Rom. 6:23). But the Bible also says that because of God's deep compassion for us, He became a man and allowed Himself to be nailed to a cross to pay the penalty for our sin (I Peter 3:18).

It's not enough just to know these great truths. We must respond to them by personal choice. The Scriptures tell us, "As many as received Him, to them He gave the right to become children of God, to those who believe in His name" (John 1:12).

Will you respond to this spiritual light God has placed before you? Right now you can go to God in prayer and express the desire of your heart. Receive the Savior's forgiveness and His gift of eternal life with Him.

It can be expressed in a simple prayer like this:
> *Jesus, I know I'm a sinner and can't save myself. Thank You*
> *for dying on the cross to pay the penalty for my sin. I receive*
> *You as my Savior and Lord. Take control of my life and make*
> *me the kind of person You want me to be.*

Did you pray that prayer? Were you sincere? If so, you can have the assurance that Jesus Christ has come into your life and given you the gift of eternal life (I John 5:12-13).

Can you think of anyone you'd like to share your new discovery with? Remember, there are people all around you who still haven't heard the saving gospel of Jesus Christ. [15]

"Life is short; death is sure, sin the curse, Christ the cure."

END NOTES

1. *"We Care News"* Volume 5, Number 2

2. Pastor George Tunks' class notes on *"Christian Humor"* held at "The Church And The Age Wave Conference," Toronto, ON, May 2001.

3. *"Youth Worker Update"* Signs of the Times, August 1993.

4. Used by permission, Bert Warden

5. Used by permission, Nina Wakelin

6. Used by permission, Brenda DiRezze

7. Used by permission, Phil Callaway www.laughagain.org.

8. Used by permission, Louise Friesen

9. Used by permission, Dr. David Lewis

10. Used by permission, Phil Callaway www.laughagain.org

11. Scripture taken from *"The Message"* (Matthew 6:34) Copyright © 1993, 1994, 1995, 1996, 2000, 2001, 2002. Used by permission of NavPress Publishing Group.

12. Reprinted from *"GrowthPoints"* with the permission of Gary L. McIntosh.

13. Used by permission, Jack Chapin

14. Used by permission, Clifford A. Olson

15. Taken from *"Our Daily Bread"* Copyright 2008 by RBC Ministries, Grand Rapids, MI. Reprinted by permission. All rights reserved.

The vast majority of the material appearing in this book is from "anonymous" or "author unknown" sources. Brief quotes do not require written permission. However, where there are names credited to larger anecdotes, attempts were made to secure permission. For the most part, I had no idea as to where to find the author or whether they were living or deceased. I spent hours on the internet trying to find the information desired. So to all those who are nameless or there is a name attached, let me say "thank you" for your contribution. Much of this material was saved when there was no thought of publishing a book, so if I do not know where a lot of it came from. That is history.

GENERAL INDEX

208

209

212

LaVergne, TN USA
08 December 2010

207830LV00002B/10/P